D1398238

ALSO BY FRED SMALL

No Limit — RNR 4018 Rounder Records
LP & Cassette
The Heart of the Appaloosa — RNR 4014 Rounder Records
LP & Cassette
Love's Gonna Carry Us — Aquifer 1001
LP & Cassette
Walk on the Supply Side — Aquifer 1002
45 RPM Single

OTHER YELLOW MOON TITLES

Music

The Magic Dulcimer; Lorraine Lee
Instructional book & tape

Storytelling Tapes

According to Tradition — Traditional Storytelling in New England; Cora Bardwell, Warren Griffin, Rosario Salve Testaverde.
Folktales of Strong Women; Doug Lipman
Maggi Peirce—Live; Maggi Peirce
A Medley of Tellers & Tales; Elizabeth Dunham, Jackson Gillman, Doug Lipman, Laura Pershin, Jay O'Callahan.

Poetry

Night & Sleep; Rumi (Translations by Coleman Barks and Robert Bly)
Body India; Elizabeth McKim
Broken Arrows; Robert Smyth

Catalog available on request with SASE

Yellow Moon Press
P.O. Box 1316
Cambridge, MA 02238

Breaking From The Line

The Songs of Fred Small

Music Transcribed & Edited
by
David Janower

Yellow Moon Press
Cambridge, Massachusetts

ISBN: 0-938756-13-3

Copyright © 1986 by Fred Small

All rights reserved. No part of this book may be reproduced or transmitted in any form or by any electronic or mechanical means including photocopying or information storage and retrieval systems without permission in writing from the publisher/copyright owner except by a reviewer who may quote brief passages in a review.

Music Notation & Calligraphy by Susan Kano
Cover Photos by Susan Wilson
Production & Design by Robert B. Smyth/Yellow Moon Press
Typesetting by Type For U, Cambridge, MA
Instigated by Marsha Cutting
Printed in the United States of America

Publication of this book was made possible in part by a grant from the Massachusetts Council on the Arts and Humanities.

Yellow Moon Press
P.O. Box 1316
Cambridge, MA 02238

The songs,
like the singing,
are dedicated to all
who by their personal acts of kindness and courage,
noticed or not, every day make a difference in the world.

PREFACE

Admittedly, I resisted Fred at first.

What chance was there, after all, that a bearded ex-lawyer with an acoustic guitar would have something significant to sing to me?

Okay, so I was wrong. And since discovering Fred Small, I've found a lot of other folks undergoing similar perception changes, encountering similar personal revelations. Some like me. Some not like me at all. Folkies who are political. Folkies who aren't. Politicos who are into folk. Politicos who aren't. Men. Women. Kids. Grandparents. Polar bears and peace dragons. In the center, left of center and, good grief, even some bright lights on the right.

What binds them, what binds *us,* all together is Fred Small, the man, the message and the music.

Music reviewers are always accused of falling back on comparisons—of the metaphor and simile sort—rather than creating original descriptions. You know the syndrome:

> He sings just like. . .
>
> Her voice is a cross between. . .
>
> Their style is reminiscent of. . .

I could fight the urge and rise above the inclination but why? Because the fact is that once I became familiar with Fred, his politics and his commitment, I could not help but think of Holly Near. No, not the musical or lyrical style, and certainly not the hair color. What Fred Small does share with Holly Near, however is a multi-faceted consciousness: an interest in, and a desire to communicate about, political, social and personal struggles that are not necessarily his own.

Fred has never been confined to a wheelchair or lost a family to an atomic bomb. He has never been a closeted lesbian schoolteacher or an overweight Italian mother. But Fred, like Holly, has gladly taken the time, the energy and the effort to dig into what other people feel, how they live—in order to find how their experiences can stretch our own realities, and can teach us to grow.

Much of Holly Near's work of course, has been adopted and nurtured by the ever-evolving women's music movement, and has become an integral part of that decade-old international circuit.

But what about Fred? Where does he fit in?

The concept of a "men's music"—music speaking to and about the sensitized, struggling contemporary male—is a vital idea. And Fred is at the forefront of an emerging group of musicians that includes Geof Morgan, Gary Lapow, Willie Sordill, Tom Wilson Weinberg and Charlie Murphy, whose music speaks to these men. Here is the beginning of what may continue to grow into a body of music and musicians that inspires men. Yet Fred's music —like Holly Near's and the best of her women's music colleagues—speaks to many others: the anti-nuclear movement, the peace movement, environmentalists, folk music lovers, lesbians and gays. In short, anyone who cares about the world we live in and our place in it.

So Fred has plenty of places to perform. For he is a singer-songwriter with political conscience and a broad world view and an entertainer with an engaging smile and an endearing, personable stage-side manner.

He's an eloquent storyteller, both in song and out. And he's a subtly persuasive preacher for open-mindedness and understanding, continually sensitizing audiences to the unfamiliar lives of others.

This last part is where Fred can, and already has made the biggest difference. His music is the stuff that builds communities, reinforces commitments and mobilizes action. Fred not only allows audiences into his music, but he encourages their participation—through singalongs, through community accessibility, through his recordings and now through this songbook.

So get out your guitars, sit down at your pianos, lift your voices and make Fred's music your own.

Susan Wilson
January, 1986

TABLE OF CONTENTS

INTRODUCTION

In 1959 a folk song was the number one song on the radio. The song was "Tom Dooley," a tragic tale of infidelity and murder which, like most folk songs, somehow sounded like fun when sung with banjo and guitar. It was performed by the Kingston Trio, three well-scrubbed college boys in matched striped shirts who offered white, middle-class America a relief from the rebellious sexuality of Elvis Presley and the black musicians he imitated.

The folk revival was on. I was six years old.

My father brought the Kingston Trio's first album into our home in the New Jersey suburbs, and I fell in love with the music. By 1960 I had saved $17.95 from my allowance to buy the worst guitar I have ever played. Within three years I was singing the songs of the Weavers, Joan Baez, Bob Dylan, and Peter, Paul, and Mary. My parents dutifully transported me to their concerts. (They loved the Weavers, but my father never did think much of Dylan's voice.)

In the early sixties, even Plainfield, New Jersey, had a coffeehouse. Having graduated to a playable instrument, I performed regularly at the open mikes, singing in my boy soprano Dylan's "Lonesome Death of Hattie Carroll," Tom Paxton's "Can't Help but Wonder Where I'm Bound" and "Daily News," Malvina Reynold's "Little Boxes" and "What Have They Done to the Rain?" and Phil Ochs's "There but for Fortune" and "Ballad of William Worthy." (I had no idea who William Worthy was, but I loved the song.) I learned much of my repertoire from *Broadside,* the topical song magazine, of which I must have been one of the youngest subscribers at age ten.

My parents were not particularly political. Although they have grown more liberal since, both voted for Eisenhower twice, and my mother voted for Richard Nixon in 1960. (By 1972, she was canvassing for McGovern.) She repeated to me what her parents had told her, that Franklin Roosevelt was "a traitor to his class." But my parents were avid supporters of their children's interests and avocations, including their son's guitar playing and singing. In 1964 we piled into the family car to drive to the Philadelphia Folk Festival. At our motel, Tom Paxton, Phil Ochs, and Gil Turner were enjoying the swimming pool. I brazenly followed Paxton to the Coke machine and struck up a conversation. When I asked his advice for a young guitarist, he suggested I work on my fingerpicking. (I did.) The next year at Philadelphia, I heard Ochs sing his stunning antiwar anthem, "I Ain't A'Marchin' Anymore." It shook me, disturbed me, made me think, and left me with an indelible impression of the power of a political song.

By the end of the 1960s the folk revival was fading as a mass phenomenon. I continued to play and sing for friends and at occasional school and college events, but my career plans were focusing on environmental law. After graduating from Yale in 1974, I entered the University of Michigan Law School. But a funny thing happened on my way to the practice of law. On the morning of my Civil Procedure examination in my first term, when I was planning to review my course outline one last time, I wrote a song about land use. It was not a good song, but it was good enough to encourage me to write another the next day, this one about energy conservation. ("Meeting America's Energy Needs," a spoof of oil company advertising that I continued to perform for several years thereafter.) Two weeks later I wrote a third song, "Death in Disguise," which was eventually recorded on my *Heart of the Appaloosa* album and is included in this book.

Although my performance on the Civil Procedure exam was nothing to write home about, I persisted in my legal studies. I left Michigan in 1978 with a J. D. and M. S. in Natural Resources Policy and Management, and after a brief stint in Denver, landed my dream job in Boston: staff attorney with the Conservation Law Foundation of New England, a regional public-interest law firm. At CLF I worked on litigation to prevent off-shore oil exploration on Georges Bank (we lost the suit but were successful in making the drilling safer), utility rate proceedings, and public recreation lands policy.

Meanwhile the music was becoming more and more exciting. In 1979 the nuclear plant at Three Mile Island nearly melted down, and the national antinuclear movement took off. I had been performing at antinuke events for years, but after TMI the rallies that had been drawing a couple of hundred people began to draw thousands and even hundreds of thousands. Although rally planners now could count on performers like Jackson Browne and Bonnie Raitt, they didn't forget me. I found myself leading vast crowds singing choruses of "Stand Up" and "Three Mile Island." Thousands of people who had never heard of me would be on their feet, singing, clapping, dancing. Most important, they would be participating in the rally—not passively consuming it as entertainment, but tapping the power of music within them. I would leave the stage feeling exhilarated, overwhelmed, privileged to have ignited that incredible human energy.

Law began to seem a little tame. Nobody applauds at oral argument. Lawyers talk mostly to other lawyers. Music was putting me in touch with all kinds of people, united in their idealism and generosity. I grew frustrated confining my music to my spare time. I decided that I could be a middle-aged lawyer any time, but if I wanted to be a musician I had better get started while I still had the enthusiasm, resilience, and minimal financial obligations. Fifteen months after starting the perfect job in environmental law, I quit.

I've never regretted it. Oh, it would have been fun to litigate against James Watt, but I sang about him instead. Instead of public-interest law, I practice public-interest music. Instead of suing to force compliance with good laws, I sing to energize people to organize to (among other things) enact the laws in the first place and to keep them on the books. Instead of persuading a judge, I persuade people from all walks of life. Instead of arguing logically from judicial precedent, I sing stories to touch people's hearts as well as minds. Instead of relying on a system of professional experts, I encourage people to take power in their lives, workplaces, and communities.

I want people to realize their innate power as artists, singers, community leaders, world-changers. I hope people will not simply reproduce my songs, but will interpret them, adding and altering words and lines and verses to meet the exigencies of the moment. I hope that my songs will encourage people to write their own, will prompt the thought: "Hey, I could write just as good a song as that."

Because I have no doubt that anyone could. This is not false modesty. Everyone has a story to tell. Everyone perceives the tragedy and hope and courage and love and humor that surround us. It is only fear and numbness and despair and poverty and oppression that prevent each and every one of us from being artists of infinite power and creativity.

To those who reach the point where they think they might possibly some day be able to write a song, I say, begin! Immediately. At the next possible moment. No more delays. No more excuses. No more listening to those ancient voices that whisper that the song won't be good enough, people will laugh, and who are we to try to write a song anyway? I have written more bad songs than good in my life, and though I have usually recognized the bad ones before inflicting them on the public, some have indeed slipped through, and I survived to learn from them. Any song that tells your story, that expresses your feelings honestly without blaming the audience, that stretches the boundaries of your craft, is a song worth writing.

Songwriting is mostly craft, I think. Some songs may leap full-grown from the brow of the muse, but most are glued painstakingly together from odd scraps of ideas and orphaned images. Keep them as simple as you can. "Any damn fool can get complicated," says Pete Seeger. "It takes genius to attain simplicity." Don't try to say everything in one song. (Songs get awfully long when you try to say everything, but some folks persist in trying.) If you can't find a new tune, borrow an old one. Woody Guthrie wrote many of his best songs that way.

Don't preach at people. Don't make them feel guilty for not doing enough: show them what's possible to do. Avoid abstract words and jargon like imperialism and sexism and exploitation, but tell stories of real people that demonstrate these problems and tell how we can get out from under them. Use an eye for detail to convey the gritty reality of the story. Sing about someone your audience will identify with and root for. Don't leave your audience informed but depressed. Leave them feeling powerful and hopeful and glad to be alive on this wonderful green earth with sisters and brothers to be cherished and defended.

Once you've written a song, sing it for friends you can trust to give you their responses and suggestions lovingly, candidly, and constructively. Don't take any one person's criticism too seriously. Almost every song I've written has displeased someone on first listening. Keep tinkering with a song till you're satisfied with it. (This may take minutes or decades.) Then sing it with all the joy and confidence and delight of a carefree child.

I hope you enjoy these songs. I've already written some more that came too late to include in this book, but these will give you a good idea of what's been on my mind the last ten years. I hope that singing these songs will help people keep moving on with courage and love and good humor to the kind of society we all deserve.

Carry it on.

Fred Small
Cambridge, Massachusetts
January, 1986

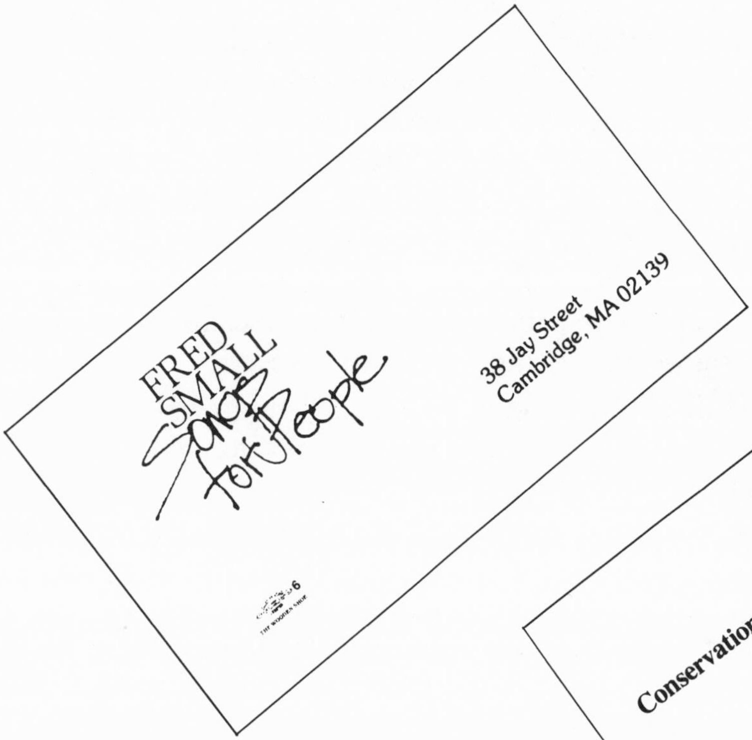

Real Life Stories

THE HEART OF THE APPALOOSA

I had just gone on break at a 1982 performance at the Idler, the legendary Cambridge folk club (now sadly gone), when a man in the audience approached me and asked if I had a moment to listen to a story. He introduced himself as John Noreika, a horsebreeder from Pennsylvania. He liked my song about Larry the Polar Bear, he said, and thought I might be interested in the story of the Appaloosa horse. He told the story briefly and it struck me powerfully as an allegory of resurrection, of rebirth, of continued struggle after apparent annihilation.

I extensively researched the historical details of the song in the library. Appaloosa horse enthusiasts confirm the story, often embellishing it with further detail, but I have also heard the claim that the role of the Appaloosa in Nez Perce history has been exaggerated and mythologized by Appaloosa owners. I can't say for sure what really happened. But if the story isn't true, it ought to be.

© 1983 Pine Barrens Music (BMI)

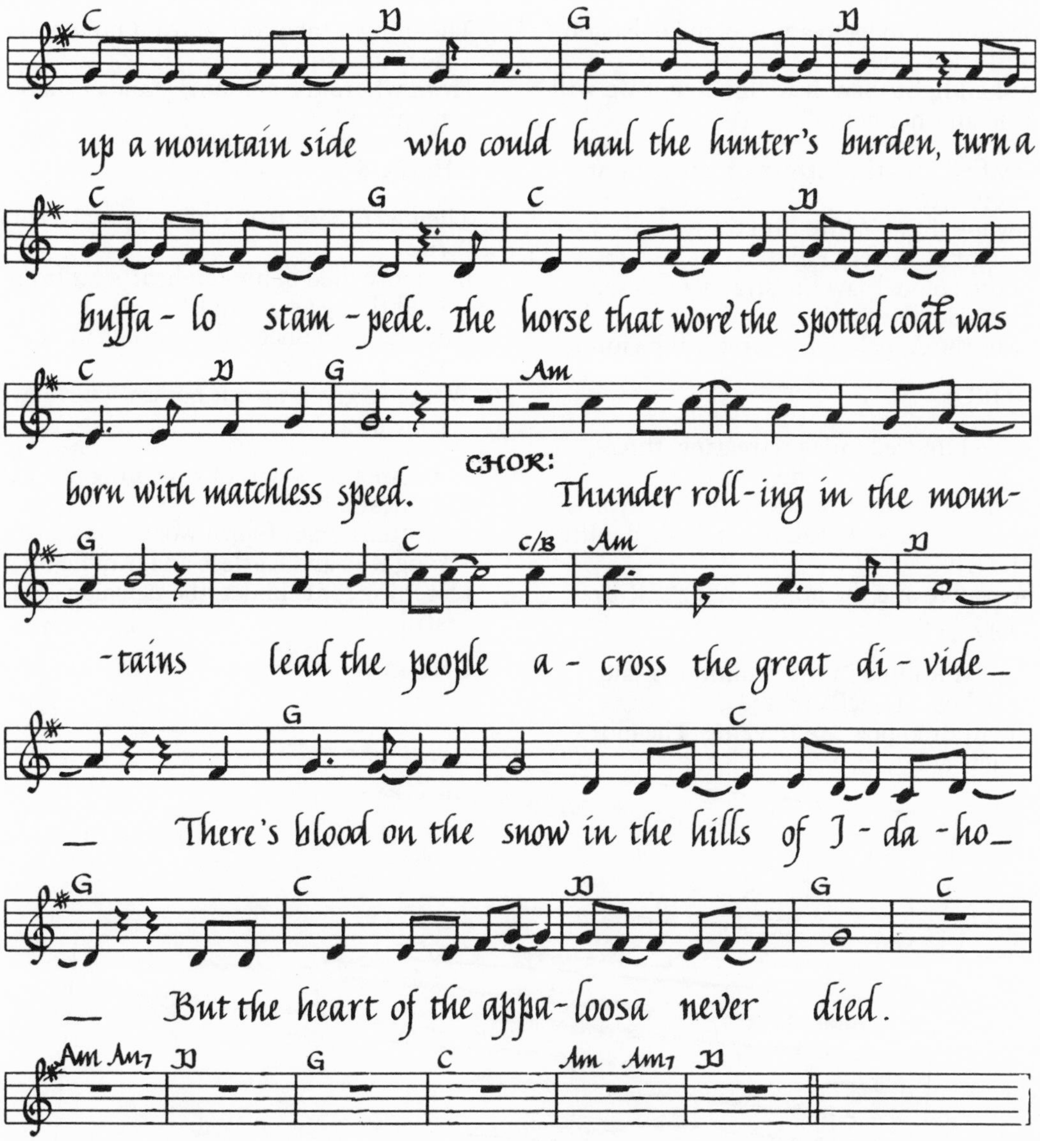

From the land of shooting waters to the peaks of the Coeur d'Alene
Thimbleberries in the forest, elk grazing on the plain
The People of the Coyote made their camp along the streams
Of the green Wallowa Valley when fences had no name.

And they bred a strain of horses, the treasure of the tribe
Who could toe-dance on a ridge or gallop up a mountainside
Who could haul the hunter's burden, turn a buffalo stampede
The horse that wore the spotted coat was born with matchless speed.

CHORUS:
Thunder Rolling in the Mountains
Lead the People across the Great Divide
There's blood on the snow in the hills of Idaho
But the heart of the Appaloosa never died.

In the winter came the crowned ones near frozen in the cold
Bringing firearms and spyglasses and a book that saves the soul
The people gave them welcome, nursed them till their strength returned
And studied the talking paper, its mysteries to learn.

In the shadow of the mission sprang up farms and squatter towns
The plain was lined with fences, the plow blade split the ground
In the shallows of the Clearwater gold glittered in the pan
And the word would come from Washington: remove the Indian.

CHORUS

The chief spoke to the People in his anger and his pain
"I am no more Chief Joseph. Rolling Thunder is my name.

They condemn us to a wasteland of barren soil and stone
We shall fight them if we must, but we will find another home."

They fled into the Bitterroot, an army at their heels
They fought at White Bird Canyon, they fought at Misery Hill
Till the colonel saw his strategy and sent the order down
To kill the Appaloosa wherever it be found.

CHORUS

Twelve hundred miles retreating, three times over the Divide
The horse their only safety, their only ally
Three thousand Appaloosas perished with the tribe
The people and the horses dying side by side.

Thunder Rolling in the Mountains said, "My heart is sick and sad.
Our children now are freezing. The old chiefs are dead.
The hunger takes our spirit. Our wounds are deep and sore.
From where the sun now stands I shall fight no more."

CHORUS

They were sent to Oklahoma, malaria ran rife
But more died of broken hearts far from the land that gave them life
And the man once called Joseph at death was heard to say
"We have given up our horses. They have gone away."

But sometimes without warning from a dull domestic herd
A spotted horse of spirit wondrous will emerge
Strong it is and fearless and nimble on a hill
Listening for thunder, the Appaloosa's living still.

CHORUS

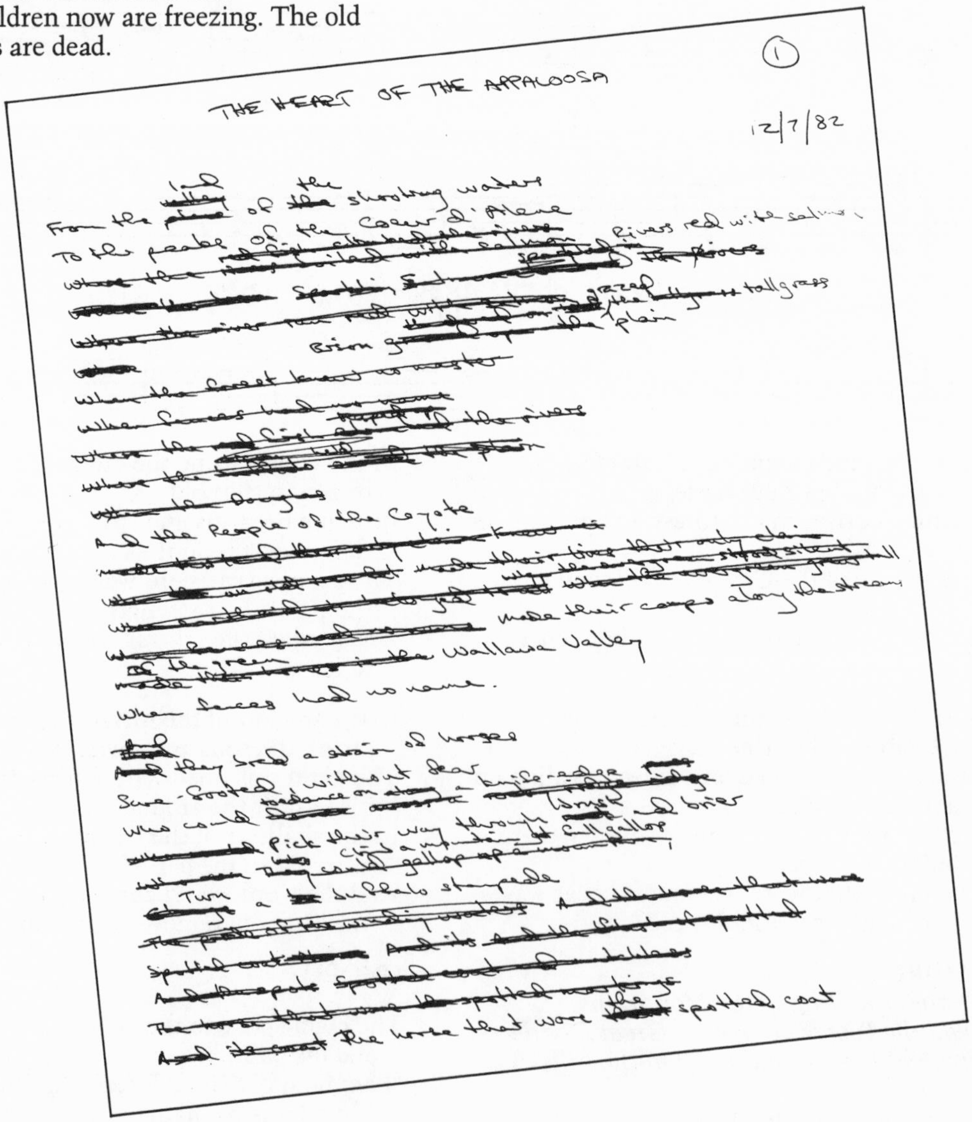

TALKING WHEELCHAIR BLUES

In 1981 my friend Meg Kocher of the Massachusetts Coalition for Citizens with Disabilities suggested I write a song about disabled people. To learn more about the subject I interviewed Meg and Rani Kronick, another friend. Meg and Rani are usually on crutches, sometimes in wheelchairs. I asked for their funny stories and their horror stories and got an earful.

I felt that a talking blues was just about the only medium for the song. Disabled people don't need another sad tale of how tragic is their fate, but I didn't think a wild comedy would go over, either. The wry irony of a talking blues reflects the attitude of many disabled people I've talked to: sometimes bitter, sometimes bemused, and determined to get their way.

© 1983 Pine Barrens Music (BMI)

I went for a jog in the city air
I met a woman in a wheelchair
I said "I'm sorry to see you're handicapped."
She says "What makes you think a thing
like that?"

And she looks at me real steady
And she says, "You want to drag?"

So she starts to roll and I start to run
And she beat the pants off my aching buns
You know going uphill I'd hit my stride
But coming down she'd sail on by!

When I finally caught up with her
She says "Not bad for somebody able-
bodied.
You know, with adequate care and
supervision
You could be taught simple tasks.
So how about something to eat?"

I said that'd suit me fine
"We're near a favorite place of mine."
So we mosied on over there
But the only way in was up a flight of stairs.

"Gee, I never noticed that," says I.
"No problem," the maitre d' replies.
"There's a service elevator around the back."

So we made it upstairs on the elevator
With the garbage, flies, and last week's potatoes
I said "I'd like a table for my friend and me."
He says "I'll try to find one out of the way."

Then he whispers, "Uh, is she gonna be sick,
I mean, pee on the floor or throw some kind of fit?"
I said " No, I don't think so,
I think she once had polio.

But that was twenty years ago.
You see, the fact of the matter is,
If the truth be told,
She can't walk.

So he points to a table, she wheels her chair
Some people look down and others stare
And a mother grabs her little girl
Says "Keep away, honey, that woman's ill."

We felt right welcome.

Then a fella walks up and starts to babble
About the devil and the holy bible
Says "Woman, though marked with flesh's sin,
Pray to Jesus, you'll walk again!"

Then the waiter says "What can I get for you?"
I said "I'll have your best imported brew."
And he says "What about her?"
I say "Who?" He says "Her."
"Oh, you mean my friend here."
He says "Yeah." I say "What about her?"
"Well, what does she want?"
"Well, why don't you ask her?"

Then he apologizes.
Says he never waited on a cripple before.
We immediately nominated him for Secretary of the Interior.

Well, she talked to the manager when we were through

She says "There're some things you could do
To make it easier for folks in wheelchairs."
He says "Oh, it's not necessary.

Handicapped never come here anyway."

Well, I said goodnight to my newfound friend
I said, "I'm beginning to understand
A little bit of how it feels
To roll through life on a set of wheels."

She says "Don't feel sorry, don't feel sad,
I take the good along with the bad
I was arrested once at a protest demo
And the police had to let me go.

See, we were protesting the fact
That public buildings weren't wheelchair accessible.
Turned out the jail was the same way.
Anyway, I look at it this way—
In fifty years you'll be in worse shape than I am now.
See, we're all the same, this human race.
Some of us are called disabled. And the rest—
Well, the rest of you are just temporarily able-bodied."

LARRY THE POLAR BEAR

This song is based on a true story. People ask what happened to Larry after he ran away. And I answer, no one knows. Maybe he survived and flourished. Maybe he died. At that moment of stunning realization of who we really are and what we must do, sometimes we must take a terrible risk. We leap into the void. But we know somehow with absolute certainty that we are going home.

When I perform "Larry the Polar Bear" with piano accompaniment (as recorded on *The Heart of the Appaloosa* album) I sing it in the key of B*b*. But when I sing it with my own guitar accompaniment, I play it in C, using these basic chords: C, Am, F, G, Em, Dm, D.

© 1983 Pine Barrens Music (BMI)

E♭ F(7) B♭
CHOR:
Lar-ry the polar bear He'd never harm a
Dm Cm F Cm F
hair on a child's head He'd do tricks for them at the Los
Cm F E♭ F Cm F B♭
Angeles zoo, as he'd been taught to by his keeper Fran.
B♭ Dm Gm Cm
Fran would teach him new tricks A funny
F Cm F B♭
pose scratching his nose He knew there'd be a fish at the
Gm F B♭ Dm
end, Fran was his friend. One day she said "Larry you'll
Gm Dm Cm F Cm
be in the movies with real movie stars and a few simple tricks
F E♭ F Cm F
and lots of fish to be filmed on lo-ca-tion in A-
E♭ C F B♭ C
laska." and so they re-hearsed for Larry's big scene, He's sup-
Dm Gm
posed to be mean and growl at a woman who was rescued by a

C F Dm
man who scared him away It was stupid but fun to
C Gm C
do. The dir-ector would frown and jump up and down —
Gm C F
kind of like the chimps at the zoo. CHOR
B♭ Dm Gm Cm
At last came the day of the trip They put Larry in a
F Cm F B♭ Dm
crate twelve foot by eight and he sailed aboard a steam-
Gm E♭ F B♭
ship The journey was long and boring Fran would
Dm Cm
visit she'd talk to him and bring him his
F E♭ C
favorite fish then the noise and the rumbling
F B♭ C F
stopped and they lowered him down set the crate on the
Dm Gm C
frozen ground and opened it

Gm C Gm
Fran said "Larry, we're here It's time for your
C4 (C3) F4 F3 Cm
tricks." And Larry appeared He looked out at the
F Gm
gray Bering Sea He squinted and puzzled
Eb F
put his nose to the wind and the scent of the seal made him
Gm Bb Gm
tremble He smelled the fox in its lair and the weasel and
F Bb
hare felt lichen and snow 'neath his paws, and he
Cm F Cm F
looked at the tundra and ice, looked at the loon in the sky and he
Gm F
ran slowly at first_
Gm F Gm
_ kind of lumbering he ran
F Eb
gathering speed gathering memories from within

Gm F
old and dim growing stronger
Gm F
to run and to swim, to dive and to float, the cold at his
Dm B♭
throat But warm in-side 'neath the fur and hide
F Cm F
— O-cean and ice all a-round him He
Gm E♭
ran He ran He
Gm F B♭
ran and he swam a-way.

LETTER FROM MAY ALICE JEFFERS

An adaptation, very nearly word for word, of a letter published in *In These Times* magazine in 1978. I have never succeeded in reaching May Alice Jeffers or her family to share the song with them. If you know how to reach them, please let me know.

I've heard some rich people say that if poor people didn't have so many children, they wouldn't be poor. This is the best rebuttal I know.

© 1981 Pine Barrens Music (BMI)

I'm an old woman typing
Old as the year, seventy-eight
Hear what I say
I was born in Laurel, Mississippi,
I live in North Carolina today
With my grandson James.

Now about the children
I had five children before the Great
Depression
Five more since then.
All of them are living now
But the one that died in the war.
All the rest had children, too.

CHORUS:
Don't blame the children
Every girl, every boy,
They ain't no burden,
They're my pride and joy.
I know they're beautiful
Like leaves on a tree
And as I am growing old
They shelter me.

I have worked at every kind of job
Nursed people, preached, and sang
When I was a young woman, I built roads
I have not worked a job
In nineteen years—my grandchildren
Take care of me.

Now listen to me
Babies don't cause poverty
'Cause poverty
Is just people never paid enough for what
we done.
You hear them talk—barefoot and
Pregnant. But I been barefoot
Pregnant or not.

CHORUS

I have known socialists
They stayed in my home in 1964
For the vote drive
They were like my children
I don't care if they be black or white
God bless you and all the socialists

My first husband was a Methodist
We did not drink but we did dance
When we had our family picnic
I think the white folks thought the colored
Was taking over, there was so many,
And the young men still ask me to dance.

CHORUS

One of Fred's first public performances as a singer-songwriter (still in law school) at The Ark Coffeehouse, Ann Arbor, MI, 1975.

LESLIE IS DIFFERENT

A true story.

© 1985 Pine Barrens Music (BMI)

The neighbor up the road brought the message
Joe and May never had a phone
Five children grown and gone to college
Now they lived out on Pewaukee Lake alone
And the nurse at the big Milwaukee hospital
Said "We've got a baby here with no eyes
It's retarded, it's got cerebral palsy
Six months old living only to die
And we remembered the tiny Englishwoman
Used to hire out as a nurse-governess
May Lemke, will you take this broken child off our hands?"
And God loves a fool 'cause she said yes. She said:

CHORUS:
Leslie is different
Like everyone in the world
He's kind of awkward, he's kind of fragile
Kind of graceful, kind of tough
He's kind of slow, he's kind of clever
He's just Leslie and that's enough.

He just lay there helpless and silent
Not a tear, not a smile, not a word
But they held him and rocked him and sang him to sleep
And talked to him as if he really heard
And he grew with the sun and affection
Though his body was spindly and small
And a hundred times they stood him with his hands upon the fence
And a hundred times watched him fall
And their daughters warned it was useless
They said, "Mama, that boy will break your heart."
She said, "Love never comes easy
And miracles mostly come hard." She said:

CHORUS

May used to play the piano
And sing the old songs from the war
There was always music on the radio
And the records she bought at the store
And sometimes they swore he was listening
Though of course there was no way to know
Maybe he was flying in his own blue sky

Where no one else would ever go
Maybe he was lost in a forest
Where demons and woodspirits dwell
But for sixteen years he had never spoke a word
Never taken one step for himself. But they said:

CHORUS

Along about three in the morning
A ripple of music broke the night
Joe's fallen asleep at the TV again
May reached over to turn on the light
But the music kept getting louder
And the TV was quiet and cold
Leslie was playing the piano
And his fingers were agile and bold
A Tchaikovsky piano concerto
Like water breaking over a dam
A river of ecstasy flowed through his hands
And each note cried out, "I am." Because

CHORUS

A MODEST PROPOSAL (THE LONG UNDERWEAR SONG)

A surefire guide to staying toasty while saving fuel. When I wrote this song in 1977, looking for a female sex star for the third verse to correspond to Newman and Redford, I chose Farrah Fawcett. Hollywood, however, discards actresses every three or four years while actors go on for decades. After recording the song with Bo Derek (her name, that is), I have since settled on Barbra Streisand as someone who's likely to be a star for a long time. Your suggestions are welcome. (Some of my friends substitute Karl Marx, Friedrich Engels, and Emma Goldman for the whole lot.)

capo up 2

© 1981 Pine Barrens Music (BMI)

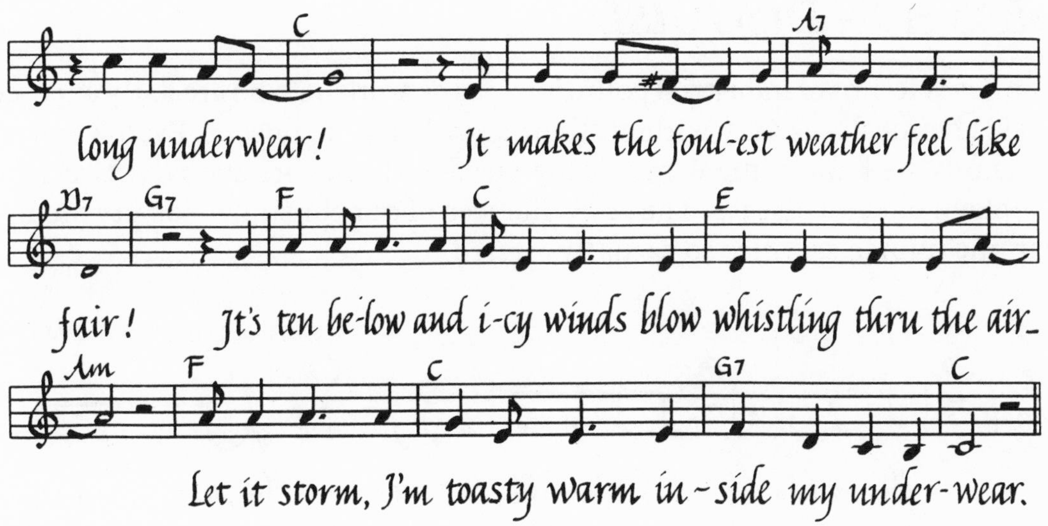

I remember well when I was but a child
of tender years
The day that I discovered the catalog
from Sears
The people in the pictures they made me
stop and stare
Who'd have guessed that they'd be dressed
in thermal underwear?

Underwear! Long underwear!
it makes the foulest weather feel like fair
It's ten below and icy winds blow whistling
through the air
Let it storm, I'm toasty warm inside
my underwear.

Prudence says to set our thermostats
at sixty-five
In skimpy briefs and brassieres you will not
survive
The Lord in all her wisdom gave us more
than skin and hair
She gave us wit, ourselves to fit with
thermal underwear.

Underwear! Long underwear!
Beneath our clothes, without it we are bare
Plutonium is perilous and coal pollutes
the air
The energy source that's best, of course, is
thermal underwear.

Paul Newman wears it all the time and
Redford he does, too
Barbra Streisand swears that it's the only
thing to do
Lovers, if you think that taking off your
clothes is nice
Do not miss the greater bliss of taking them
off twice!

Underwear! Long underwear!
Slip inside and leave behind your cares
The oil and gas kingpins will rant and tear
their hair
Who needs them? We've got a friend in
thermal underwear.

". . . beware of all enterprises that require new clothes. . ."

—Henry David Thoreau, *Walden*

DEATH IN DISGUISE

The first victims of industrial pollution are the workers who are daily exposed to toxic chemicals, usually without their knowledge or consent. Even when the hazards are known, many people are faced with the dire choice between unemployment and disease. The conveniences of our consumer society are not worth the human sacrifice so casually offered.

© 1983 Pine Barrens Music (BMI)

All my life
Working at the factory
The pay looked mighty good to me
When my body was my own
Doctor won't look me in the eye
My youngest child asks why
I won't ever see her grown.

CHORUS:
Now I can feel the darkness
Growing wild inside me
Catching my soul by surprise
You know that you've made it
You got your home, your job, and some good times
Then they tell you it was death in disguise.

In the consultation room
They explain the x-ray slide
I stop the rising tide
Of self-pity and cold fear
Pale in the fluorescent light
I find no one left to fight
And remember all my careless years.

CHORUS

Half the town works there
So people fear the truth
There's no conclusive proof
There's any danger in those fumes
The company never saw my face
They've got another in my place
Another life to be consumed.

CHORUS

"I think real folk stuff scares most of the boys around Washington. A folk song is what's wrong and how to fix it, or it could be who's hungry and where the mouth is, or who's out of work and where the job is or who's broke and where the money is or who's carrying a gun and where the peace is—that's folk lore and folks made it up because they seen that the politicians couldn't find nothing to fix or nobody to feed or give a job of work."

—Woody Guthrie

THREE MILE ISLAND

The nuclear industry is surely a dinosaur in the ice age, but a lot of cave men with a lot of money at stake are trucking in little quartz heaters to fend off the inevitable, and sending us the bill. Meanwhile, they export reactors to the Third World. As Michio Kaku likes to say—"Shut 'em down!"

© 1981 Pine Barrens Music (BMI)

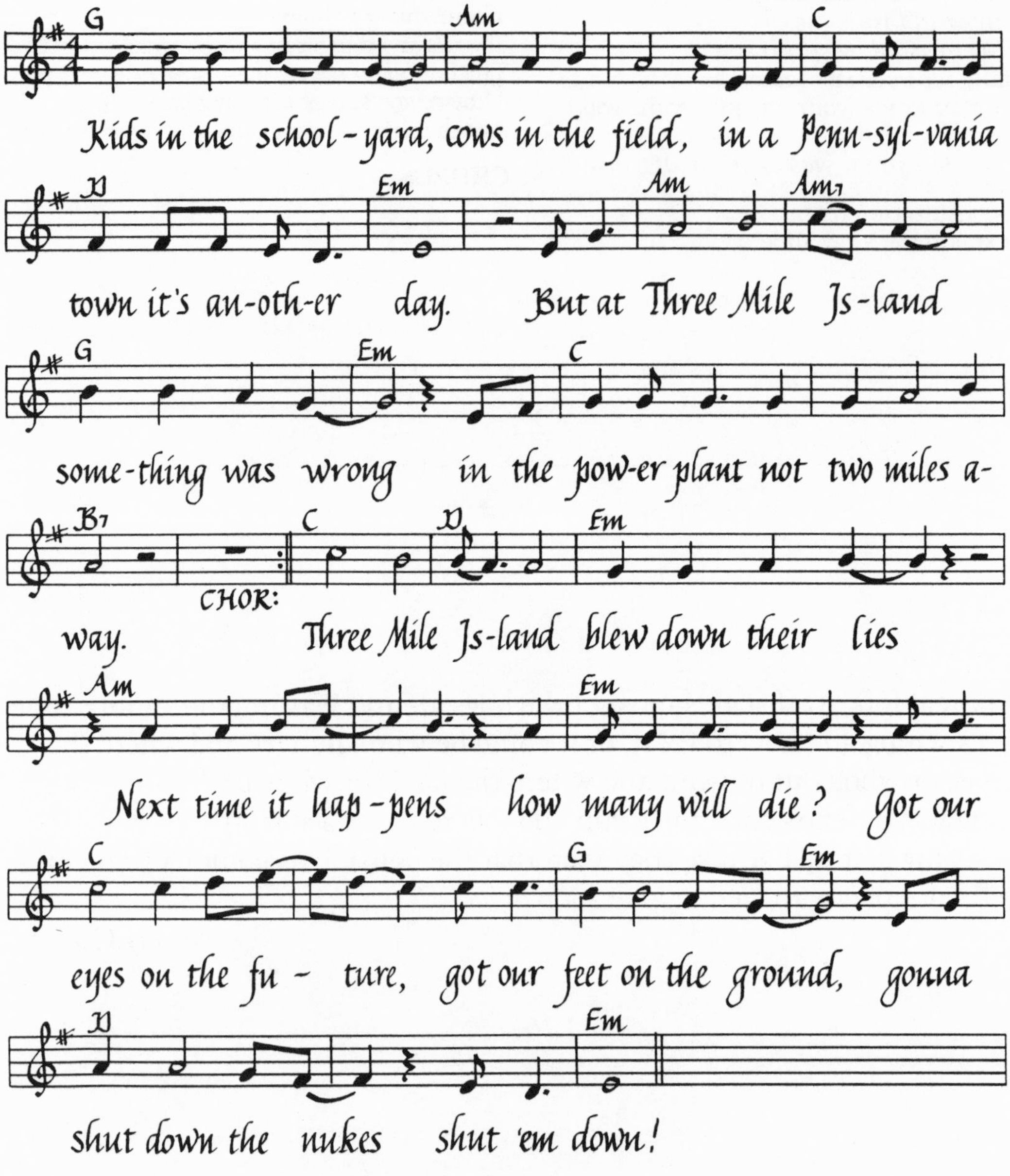

Kids in the schoolyard, cows in the field
In a Pennsylvania town it's another day
But at Three Mile Island something was wrong
In the power plant not two miles away.

A valve jammed open and the holding tanks blew
And the leak spread for miles around.
With a bubble of hydrogen trapped under the dome
That plant damn near melted down.

CHORUS:
Three Mile Island blew down their lies
Next time it happens how many will die?
Got our eyes on the future, got our feet on the ground
Gonna shut down the nukes, shut 'em down
Shut down the nukes, shut 'em down.

Metro Edison said one thing, the feds the reverse
The TV and press had their fun
Out of all the confusion just one thing came through
No one knew what the hell was going on.

Evacuation would have ended the game
So they said there was no reason to go
But they didn't say too much about the workers at the plant
Who as always caught the brunt of the blow.

CHORUS

The sun it shines, the wind it blows
There's a thousand different ways to save fuel
So when some corporation tells me we got no choice
They might as well be calling me a fool.

They say the system worked and no one was killed
They say they'll make 'em safer than before
But they're gambling with our children and they're gambling with the world
And their money don't seem worth dying for.

CHORUS

1981

PRINGLE JINGLE

A smash hit at elementary schools where I perform, this is a hymn to an intrepid pioneer on the frontier of food technology. Since 1975, when the song was written, BHA has been removed from Pringles—but sugar has been added!

© 1975 Fred Small

CHORUS:
Pringle's Newfangled
Potato Chips!
They're crunchy, so munchy,
They'll make you smack your lips.
Boon to the consumer,
Triumph for man,
To fit so many potato chips
In a tennis ball can!

A misshapen potato chip
Can ruin your whole day.
Ours are perfect ovals,
Identical in every way.
None is too greasy,
None is too brown.
Our rehydrated potatoes
Make the best chips in town!

CHORUS

Four and one-half ounces
Only eighty-seven cents—
We only use the finest
Ingredients.
Mono- and diglycerides,
BHA—
They can sit on the shelf for nineteen weeks
And you can buy them anyway!

CHORUS

All this may sound incredible,
But wait—there's even more:
You can take our chip where potato chips
Have never been before!
Stuff 'em in your knapsack,
Not one will break.
And you can leave the can at the campsite
Or floating in the lake!

CHORUS

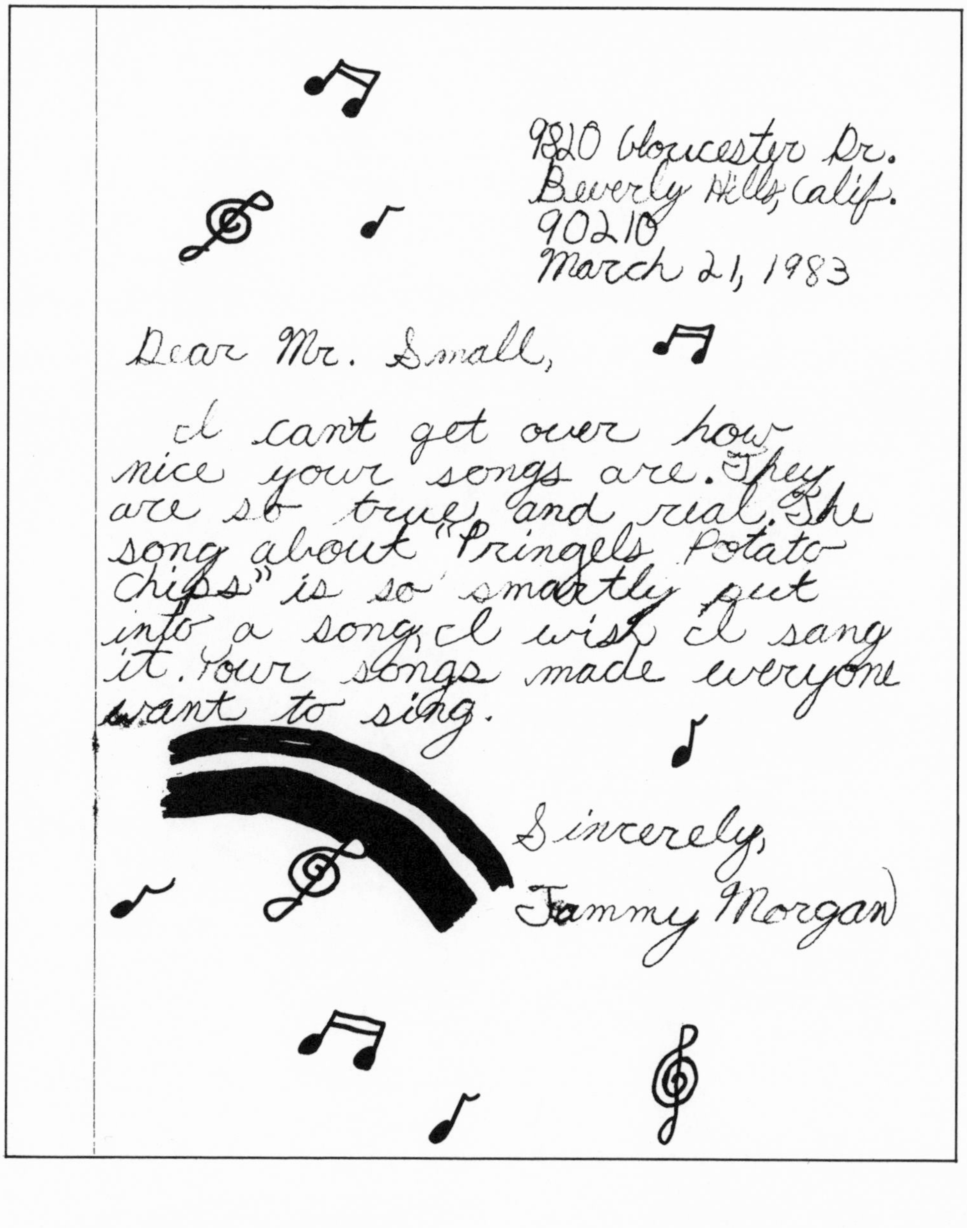
9810 Gloucester Dr.
Beverly Hills, Calif.
90210
March 21, 1983

Dear Mr. Small,

I cant get over how nice your songs are. They are so true and real. The song about "Pringels Potato Chips" is so smartly put into a song I wish I sang it. Your songs made everyone want to sing.

Sincerely,
Tammy Morgan

Songs of Changing Women & Men

FIFTY-NINE CENTS

Women are paid fifty-nine cents for every dollar that men are paid, on the average. That statistic varies slightly from year to year and state to state, but not much. (When they change the button, I'll change the song!)

© 1981 Pine Barrens Music (BMI)

High school daydreams come easy and free
When you're a working woman watcha
gonna be?
A senator, a surgeon, aim for the heights
But the guidance office says lower your
sights to

CHORUS:
Fifty-nine cents for every man's dollar
Fifty-nine cents it's a lowdown deal
Fifty-nine cents makes a grown woman
holler
They give you a diploma it's your paycheck
they steal.

She's off to college, the elite kind
To polish her manners, sharpen her mind
Honors in English, letter in lacrosse
Types her to type for her favorite boss at

CHORUS *(They give you a degree . . .)*

Junior executive on her way up
Special assistant to the man at the top
She's one in a million and all she found
Was her own secretary now to order
around at

CHORUS *(They give you a title . . .)*

But the word is being processed in the typing pool
A working woman ain't nobody's fool
She's telling the boss on Secretary's Day
You can keep your flowers, buddy, give me a raise more than

CHORUS
Fifty-nine cents for every man's dollar
Fifty-nine cents—oh, the deal has changed
Fifty-nine cents makes a grown woman holler
You can keep your flowers, buddy, give us a raise.

"This song is Copyrighted in U.S. under Seal of Copyright #154085, for a period of 28 years, and anybody caught singin' it without our permission, will be mighty good friends of our'n, cause we don't give a dern. Publish it. Write it. Sing it. Swing to it. Yodel it. We wrote it, that's all we wanted to do."

—Woody Guthrie

THE HUG

A true story. A hug, freely given and freely received, is one of nature's delights. (But look out for mashers in "hug therapist" t-shirts.) The additional lyrics are for young people who might not understand electroshock and sexual sublimation. (But then, who does?)

Capo up 2

© 1981 Pine Barrens Music (BMI)

Dan Murrow is a mighty friendly man
He's big and round like a bear
He hugs his friends and his friends hug him
Anytime, anywhere.
His patients would come for therapy
To drive their blues away
And sooner or later they'd feel a lot better
Cause this is what he'd say:

CHORUS:
I want a hug when we say hello
I want a hug when it's time to go
I want a hug 'cause I want you to know
I'm awfully fond of you.
I want a hug—what a wonderful feeling
I want a hug—to feel you squeezing
I want a hug—it certainly seems like
The natural thing to do!

But when the head of the hospital heard about it
He got all annoyed
Cause hugging is sexual sublimation
According to Doctor Freud.
You can beat 'em down, you can hide 'em away,
You can keep 'em quiet with drugs,
You can strap 'em and zap 'em with electroshock
But you better not give 'em a hug.

CHORUS

So the boss says, "Dan, clean out your desk—
Your conduct is lax and lewd.
Any deviation from standard medical
Practice can get us sued."
Now, Dan don't feel too bad for himself
He's really kind of proud.
But he's sorry for the people who are locked away
Where hugging ain't allowed.

CHORUS

© 1984 Pine Barrens Music (BMI)

CHORUS
When I was a little bitty baby child, my momma used to hold me tight
My daddy used to come and pick me up when I got scared at night
The years have passed, I've grown so fast, and mostly I feel strong
But timid or bold, I'm never too old to sing this cozy song.

CHORUS

Now some folks don't like hugging—they think they're too tough
I bet they'd be a whole lot friendlier if they were just hugged enough
When you hug the ones who love you, an amazing thing you learn
When you give a hug, you just can't help but get one in return!

CHORUS

Sometimes grownups are grouchy and they put the blame on you
Sometimes you make just a little mistake though you did the best you could do
Sometimes love is everywhere and it's a beautiful day
And every time is the perfect time to open your arms and say:

CHORUS

ANNIE

I wrote this song primarily for people who have never attended a women's music concert. I wrote it for people who may not have given much thought to what it's like to live in a closet day after day, kept there for fear of losing one's job, one's children, one's life. The song supports gays and lesbians in the choices, sometimes difficult and compromised, they make in their lives.

© 1983 Pine Barrens Music (BMI)

Annie's up at seven on a work day
Brewing up a cup of peppermint tea
Gathering her papers and lesson plans
She grabs her keys
Teaching arithmetic and Africa
Geology and girls' basketball
All the kids in her class
Will tell you she's the best
But she's heard other teachers in the hall
saying

CHORUS:
"What are we going to do about Annie?
Pretty girl like her shouldn't be alone
If she took our advice, dressed up real nice
She'd find a man to take her home."

Mondays come with questions of couples
Where and with whom did you go?
Avoiding the personal pronoun
She hopes it doesn't show
Shopping with her lover in the city
Two women holding hands don't get a stare
If the kids at school knew what would they
do
Would they hate her? Why should they care?
Tell me

CHORUS

Never getting too close to a student
Never letting out too much of her life
Keeping her delights and disappointments
Tucked out of sight
Annie takes herself to the Christmas party
The principal whispers with a smile
"You're vivacious and bright, if you play
your cards right
There're some men here tonight worth your
while" thinking

CHORUS

Work that you love is hard to come by
The kids she could never bear to lose
So she makes conversation out of silences
And half-truths
But at night by the fire with her lover
She looks out at the wind-driven snow
And imagines the day when she'll look in
their faces
And tell everybody she knows—she'll tell
'em

LAST CHORUS:
Don't you worry about Annie
She don't lie awake and pine
Got love to fill her heart, flowers growing in
the garden
Annie's doing just fine.

"Every folk song was a topical song at its birth, a comment upon the life and times of singers and listeners."

—Pete Seeger, *The Incompleat Folksinger*

FATHER'S SONG

A wall of awkwardness and fear separates many fathers and sons, but love abides. Many men are reaching out to their fathers and their sons to find out what it's really been like for them.

© 1985 Pine Barrens Music (BMI)

I remember the man
Rising early in the morning
Smelling of starch and aftershave
Sometimes I would shave beside him
With a plastic razor and a cardboard blade
And watch his car disappear
Into the morning gray.

I remember the man
Talking so long on the telephone
His voice hard and polished like a precious
stone
In command of itself and the darkness
He was not afraid in my hearing
Though sometimes he would rage
Without reason.

CHORUS:
There's a man I hardly remember
Who would hold me in his arms without
flinching
And tell me it's all right
I put my hands out to my father
Standing strong in the water
When I could not swim
I held on to him
It was all right.

I remember the man
Shouting from the sidelines at my football
games
He'd razz opposing players by their names
My mother would plead, Oh please calm
down

And he did when the game was over
He was so proud
Of his son.

I remember the man
Laid off last December
That's not what they called it
Twenty years with the firm
Eased out in favor of a younger man
Fear tugged at his voice
But he had other plans.

CHORUS

I dreamed last night of my grandmother
She was tall and I a child
But death was hiding in her house
In the dark I saw her
A rotting shell
And I cried out
My father took my hand
And led me from that awful place.

Soon my parents will be old
They will count their dreams and weight
them
One by one
Two lives long together, a daughter and a
son
Many things accomplished, many left
undone
Some left behind
For something better.

And once before he dies
I will hold him in my arms without
flinching
And tell him it's all right
I put my hands out to my father
Standing strong in the water
When I could not swim
I held on to him
It was all right.

Fred and his father, Roger Small, Indian Hill summer arts camp, 1967.

Photo: Todd Gipstein

Roger Small at one of Fred's football games, 1969.

BIG ITALIAN ROSE

In the nineteenth century, many women wore corsets, which were expensive, time-consuming, and painful but which kept them thin. A hundred years later, thank heavens, women have stopped wearing corsets. Instead, many women go to aerobics classes, which are expensive, time-consuming, and painful but which keep them thin. (With men's liberation, men are free to take on the same compulsions that women have enjoyed for years.) Multimillion dollar industries exist solely on the premise that each of us should actually look like somebody else.

The point of the song is not that being fat is better than being thin (or vice versa), and it is certainly not that Italian women are fat. The point of the song is that whatever size, shape, or configuration you happen to find yourself in, it's probably just fine, so you may as well relax and enjoy it.

I first heard this story second-hand and immediately sat down and wrote the song. When I got the story first-hand I discovered that it had been changed a little in the telling, but the basics were true. So I kept the song according to the rumor.

© 1985 Pine Barrens Music (BMI)

She was riding on the airline leafing through
their magazine
They said, "We'll fly you to the homeland
that you have never seen"
Smiling tourists in the picture back in
sunny Italy
Said she, "These pretty people don't look
anything like me!"

CHORUS:

*"I'm a big Italian woman and I want the
world to see
All the big Italian women who look just
like me
You can take your slender models and their
Fifth Avenue clothes
But you'll never find a flower like the big
Italian rose!"*

Well, the more she thought about it, the
more it made her mad
How they make you feel so ugly, they make
you feel so bad
Sell you junk food and booze then make
you diet till you're dead
She sat and wrote a letter and this is what
it said:

CHORUS

"Well, I'm nearly fifty-seven, my hair is
turning gray
The dress I wore at twenty I cannot wear
today
Just an ordinary woman and it sure would
make me glad
Just for once to see someone like me in your
ad."

CHORUS

Three weeks later came an answer, from
New York it was sent
Said "We'd like to take your picture for our
next advertisement."
Soon magazines across the nation in a
prominent place
Showed a big Italian woman with a smile on
her face.

CHORUS

JIMMY COME LATELY

Based on the story of Phil Woolpert, who coached the University of San Francisco basketball team to several NCAA championships in the 1950s with players like Bill Russell and K. C. Jones. Then, at an age when many coaches are negotiating million-dollar contracts, Phil retired to Sequim, Washington, to drive a school bus. Jimmy Come Lately Road and Lost Mountain Road are streets in Sequim. Phil's story appealed to me as an example of a man seeing through the success trap and going after the life he wants.

© 1985 Pine Barrens Music (BMI)

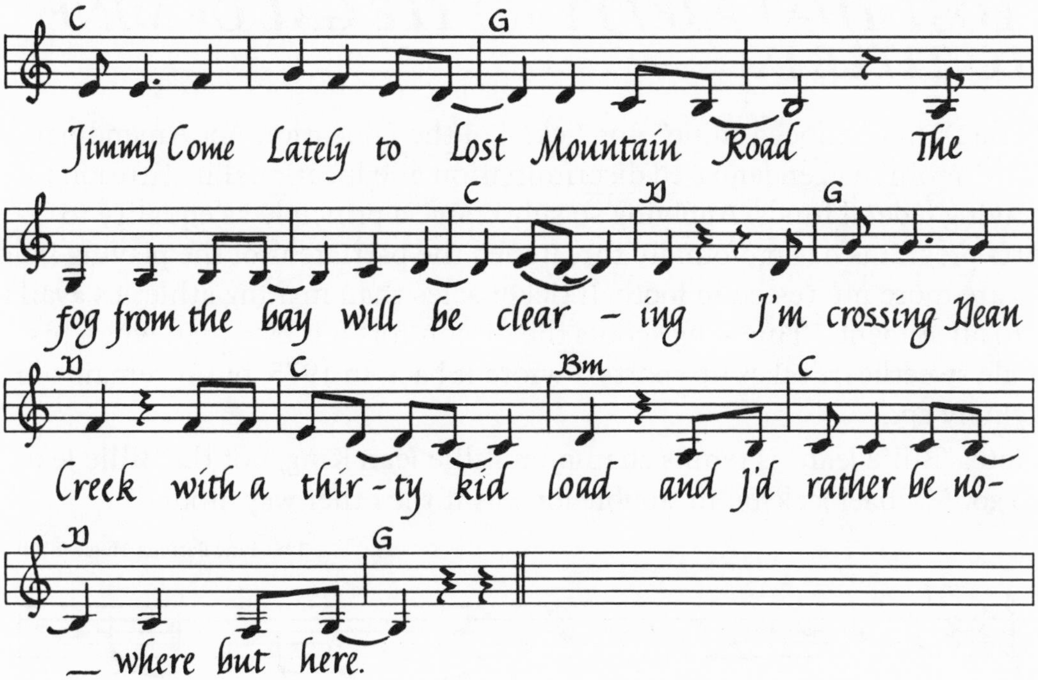

I pull out the choke, pump hard on the gas
Oh, this wheezing old bus is complaining
The Dungeness winter is blowing its last
It's cold but for once it's not raining.
"Good morning, Jennifer, welcome aboard
That's a handsome new jacket you're
wearing
Now hustle up, Carrie, I'm closing the door
And I'll ask you to knock off the swearing."

CHORUS:
*And it's Jimmy Come Lately to Lost
Mountain Road*
The fog from the bay will be clearing
*I'm crossing Dean Creek with a thirty-kid
load*
And I'd rather be nowhere but here.

I can still smell the sweat, hear the cry of
the crowd
And the team on the magazine covers
My wallet was thick, the airports were loud
Till the Monday I knew it was over
My back had gone out and I lay awake
nights
As I diagrammed plays on the ceiling
All the motel room calls to my
long-distance wife
Made me feel like a junkie caught stealing.

CHORUS

I've seen TV lights turn a good coach mean
Seen the pressure break a family apart
I grabbed for the glory, I wore the gold ring
And I barely escaped with my heart
Now Patrick Delaney — I've seen the kid
play
God, he's got the moves and the shooting
He's already talking 'bout U.C.L.A.
While the agents line up for the looting.

CHORUS

Now Mary and me, we're a comfortable fit
And the ocean here's running with salmon
Evenings we take a long walk on the spit
And Sundays sometimes we go clamming
And they still make me offers and I just
turn 'em down
It's a wonder they bother to find me
I'll leave to Valvano and Lewis and Brown
The wonders that I left behind me.

CHORUS

I LOST THAT PRETTY LITTLE GAL OF MINE (TO TITLE IX)

Title IX (pronounced "nine", not "icks") of the Education Act Amendments of 1972 prohibits gender-based discrimination at educational institutions receiving federal funds. Applying so subversive a principle as equality to sports programs has profoundly threatened the patriarchs of the playing fields who are more interested in football ticket sales than making athletics available to all students. This song spoofs the discomfort felt by a man when his female sweetheart takes up sports. I wrote it back in 1975, but it remains dismayingly apt.

Note: "Billie Jean" is tennis champion Billie Jean King, not the Billie Jean who got Michael Jackson in trouble (or was it the other way around?).

© 1981 Pine Barrens Music (BMI)

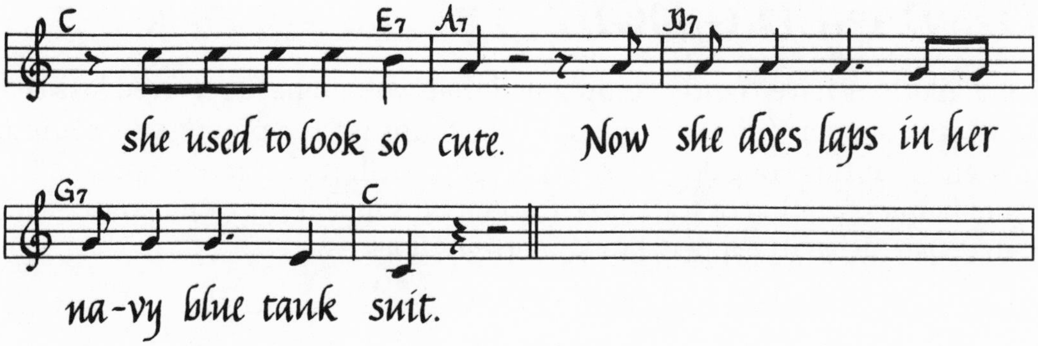

I lost that pretty little gal of mine to
Title IX
I found her in the stands but I lost her at the
finish line
She was so soft and sweet
But now I find I can't compete
I lost that gal of mine to Title IX.

Sure, I put my money on Billie Jean.
But that damn King has taken away my
queen.
She learned a new topspin
Now she won't let me win
She doesn't want me on her doubles team.

Her old letters made my heart melt
Now they're on her sweater and they're
made of felt
In her bikini she used to look so cute
Now she does laps in her navy blue tank suit.

She does windsprints, I do the wash
I stuff zucchini while she's playing squash
On a date I'm so tense
She's itchin' to try her self defense
And violence I cannot bear to watch.

Her old soft spots are hard today
The problem I've got's just the other way
She used to cheer me as I ran my race
Now I find I can't keep her pace.

FRED SMALL: Love's Gonna Carry Us (Aquifer) This 1981 LP reaches far beyond its grasp. It's essentially an album of topical folk songs, which, aside from being unfashionable, means that the message overshadows the medium. As with much so-called "women's music," the result is bland (or worse) music and baldly simplistic lyrics. Small's thin, plaintive voice and awkward phrasing make his words that much more embarrassing. His attempts at humor fail completely. Even worse is that while this is a mainly acoustic recording, some overtly commercial "rock" arrangements make a few songs totally unbearable.—Scott Becker

OP—Independent Music Magazine, Jan.–Feb. '84

THE DANCING LIGHT

Some mothers have rightly complained that women have received less than enthusiastic support for parenting from the feminist and progressive communities, and that this song doesn't seem to help. Still, it accurately conveys the sad and helpless feeling of watching a woman disappear into a marriage—which doesn't have to happen, but sometimes does.

Capo up 2

© 1981 Pine Barrens Music (BMI)

I remember her when she was
shining bright
Deep in her dark eyes there shone a
dancing light
She always used to say that she was not the
marrying kind
Until she met the man who changed
her mind

He was beautiful and Lord he was strong
Knew where he was going, rising like
the sun
And he believed in her and listened to
her thoughts
And long into the evening they would talk.

CHORUS:
Seemed like we just blinked our eyes and
she slipped away
This woman full of fire and wonder only
yesterday
There ain't no doubt she's happy, ain't
nothing really wrong
But the dancing light inside her eyes is gone.

He got the job he wanted, she left
hers behind
She said she had no future there, she
didn't mind.
In another city she began a brand new life
Loving the man and learning to be a wife

We still get a letter from time to time
She writes about the baby, not what's on
her mind.
I guess she's got her reasons, it ain't for me
to say
But it makes me sad to lose a friend that way.

CHORUS

But the dancing light inside her eyes—
It's hard sometimes just to survive—
Oh the dancing light is gone.

ARE YOU KAREN SILKWOOD?

In 1974, union activist Karen Silkwood drove to a meeting with a New York Times reporter about safety problems at the plutonium reprocessing plant where she worked. She never reached her destination. She was found dead in the wreck of her Honda Civic. State police ruled it an accident, but an investigator for the Oil, Chemical & Atomic Workers determined that she had been forced off the road. Silkwood's courage has inspired those concerned about the safety of the nuclear fuel cycle and the working people who are its first victims.

© 1976 Fred Small

Are you Karen Silkwood?
The news is bad—
Your body's on fire,
The worst that we've had.
Might have been the canister,
Probably the gloves.
Better not get too near
To the ones that you love.

Are you Karen Silkwood?
We've heard about you.
Talkin' to the outside—
Dumb thing to do.
People lose confidence,
We might close down.
Little girl, the stakes are high—
We don't fool around.

Are you Karen Silkwood?
Baby, come to bed.
This thing's too big for us;
It's gone to your head.
You've got your mission,
I've got my doubts.
I never asked for this—
Babe, I think I want out.

Are you Karen Silkwood?
I'll be on the next flight.
I think we've got 'em nailed this time—
Are you sure you're all right?
The union's behind you
Right down the line.
I'll be there at the restaurant
With the man from the Times.

Are you Karen Silkwood?
Christ, there's nothin' but blood.
Better get the ambulance,
But it won't do no good.
They're sayin' she had some notes in the car,
But they're nowhere around.
Shit, the place is crawlin' with press—
But she don't make a sound.

Photo: James G. Smerecak

1981

EVERYTHING POSSIBLE

A lesbian friend of mine asked me to write a song she could sing to her nine-year-old son about the choices we can make about how to live and whom to love. The next day, on a rainy bus ride from Seattle to Olympia, this song came to me. (When Priscilla Herdman recorded the song with me for my *No Limit* album, she was eight months pregnant! I hope the song stays with her daughter, Suzanna.)

© 1983 Pine Barrens Music (BMI)

G A D D
love whom-ev-er you will You can travel a-ny
A G A G A
country where your heart leads and know I will love you
D D Bm
still You can live by your-self you can
Em7 A G Em7
gather friends a-round you can choose one special one
A D A G
— and the on-ly measure of your words and your deeds
A G A D
— will be the love you leave be-hind when you're done
A Bm F#
BRIDGE:
Don't be rat-tled by names, by taunts, by
G D
games, but seek out spir-its true If you
G F#m
give your friends the best part of your-self they will
Em7 G Em7 A
— give the same back to you. You can

We have cleared off the table, the leftovers saved
Washed the dishes and put them away
I have told you a story and tucked you in tight
At the end of your knockabout day
As the moon sets its sails to carry you to sleep
Over the midnight sea
I will sing you a song no one sang to me.
May it keep you good company.

CHORUS:
You can be anybody you want to be
You can love whomever you will
You can travel any country where your heart leads
And know I will love you still
You can live by yourself, you can gather friends around
You can choose one special one
And the only measure of your words and your deeds
Will be the love you leave behind when you're done.

There are girls who grow up strong and bold
There are boys quiet and kind
Some race on ahead, some follow behind
Some go in their own way and time
Some women love women, some men love men
Some raise children, some never do
You can dream all the day never reaching the end
Of everything possible for you.

Don't be rattled by names, by taunts, by games
But seek out spirits true
If you give your friends the best part of yourself
They will give the same back to you.

CHORUS

Peace is the Bread We Break

PEACE IS

Even in the shadow of death, we hold the power of love and the promise of life. I dedicate this song to everyone who has marched in the rain, stuffed envelopes, made phone calls, gone to jail, or lifted their voice in song to safeguard this fragile earth for those who will inherit it.

© 1983 Pine Barrens Music (BMI)

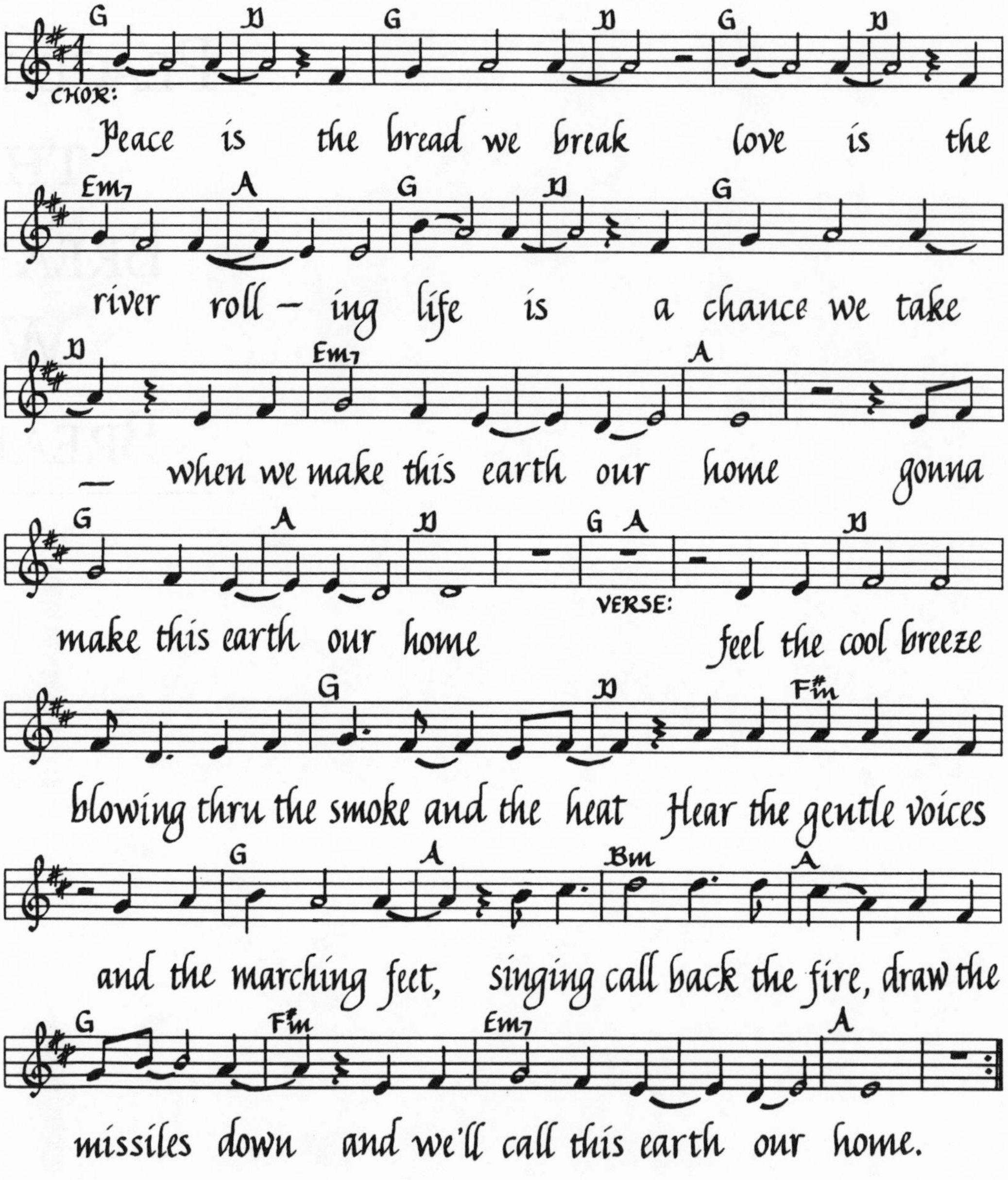

Feel the cool breeze blowing through the smoke and the heat
Hear the gentle voices and the marching feet
Singing call back the fire, draw the missiles down
And we'll call this earth our home.

CHORUS:
Peace is the bread we break
Love is the river rolling
Life is a chance we take
When we make this earth our home
Gonna make this earth our home.

We have known the atom, the power and pain
We've seen people fall beneath the killing rain
If the mind still reasons and the soul remains
It shall never be again.

CHORUS

Peace grows from a tiny seed
As the acorn grows into the tallest tree
Many years ago I heard a soldier say
When people want peace, better get out of the way.

CHORUS

Photo: Ellen Shub

1985

CRANES OVER HIROSHIMA

Sadako Sasaki, a child in Hiroshima, survived the atom blast but grew sick from the radiation. Following a Japanese tradition that holds that folding a thousand origami cranes will bring good health, she began making paper cranes. On the base of her statue in the Hiroshima Peace Park is this inscription: "This is our cry. This is our prayer. Peace in the world."

© 1983 Pine Barrens Music (BMI)

The baby blinks her eyes as the sun falls from the sky
She feels the stings of a thousand fires as the city around her dies
Some sleep beneath the rubble, some wake to a different world
From the crying babe will grow a laughing girl.

Ten summers fade to autumn, ten winters' snows have passed
She's a child of dreams and dances, she's a racer strong and fast
But the headaches come ever more often and the dizziness always returns
And the word that she hears is leukemia and it burns.

CHORUS:

Cranes over Hiroshima, white and red and gold
Flicker in the sunlight like a million vanished souls
I will fold these cranes of paper to a thousand one by one
And I'll fly away when I am done.

Her ancestors knew the legend—if you make a thousand cranes
From squares of colored paper, it will take the pain away
With loving hands she folds them, six hundred forty-four
Till the morning her trembling fingers can't fold anymore.

CHORUS

Her friends did not forget her—crane after crane they made
Until they reached a thousand and laid them upon her grave
People from everywhere gathered, together a prayer they said
And they wrote the words in granite so none can forget:

This is our cry, this is our prayer, peace in the world.

THE PEACE DRAGON

Marissa Betz-Zall, a five-year-old Philadelphian, told me about the peace dragon. When I asked her what the peace dragon eats, she replied, "cruise missiles."

Capo up 4

© 1983 Pine Barrens Music (BMI)

The peace dragon sleeps in a cave in a cliff
on a crystal sea
It wakes when sunlight slips inside with a
fine good morning breeze
Then it snaps its tail and cracks its claws
and beats its giant wings
And it rides the rivers of the sky and peace
to all it brings.

CHORUS:
*Oh it snaps its tail and cracks its claws and
beats its giant wings
and it rides the rivers of the sky and peace
to all it brings.*

For breakfast it likes nothing more than missiles that go crunch
A nuclear submarine sandwich really hits the spot for lunch
For dessert perhaps a neutron bomb washed down with a chemical brew
Digesting deadly weapons seems a peaceful thing to do.

CHORUS

The general stamped his foot and swore he'd slay that lizard of peace
He launched a secret rocket while the dragon lay sound asleep
But friendly bats with sonar ears their serpent pal awoke
And one quick snort from a fiery snout sent the rocket right up in smoke.

CHORUS

Children wave and shout hello when it flies overhead
It calls to people, "Please don't fight but think and talk instead
Don't send your young ones off to war, don't poison all the earth
When you're truly big and strong you'll understand what peace is worth."

CHORUS

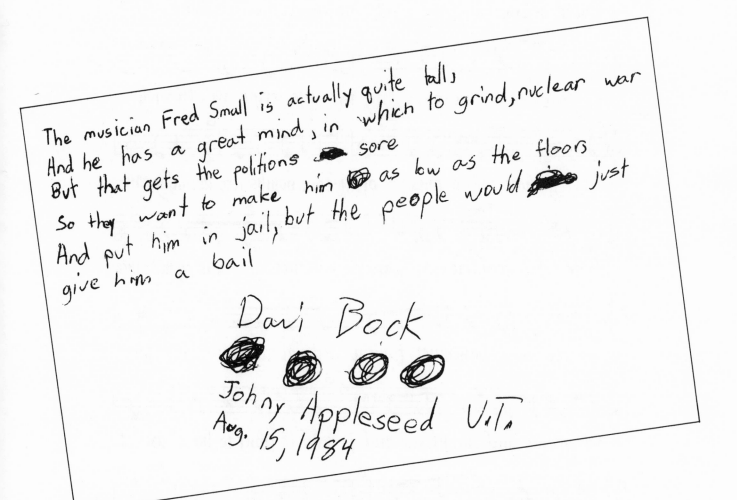

The musician Fred Small is actually quite tall,
And he has a great mind, in which to grind, nuclear war
But that gets the politions sore
So they want to make him as low as the floors
And put him in jail, but the people would just
give him a bail

Davi Bock

Johnny Appleseed V.T.
Aug. 15, 1984

DIG A HOLE IN THE GROUND

Based on the immortal words of T. K. Jones, President Reagan's Deputy Undersecretary of Defense: "Dig a hole, cover it with a couple of doors and then throw three feet of dirt on top . . . It's the dirt that does it . . . if there are enough shovels to go around, everybody's going to make it." Proving again the old maxim that some folks you don't have to satirize, you just quote 'em.

© 1982 Pine Barrens Music (BMI)

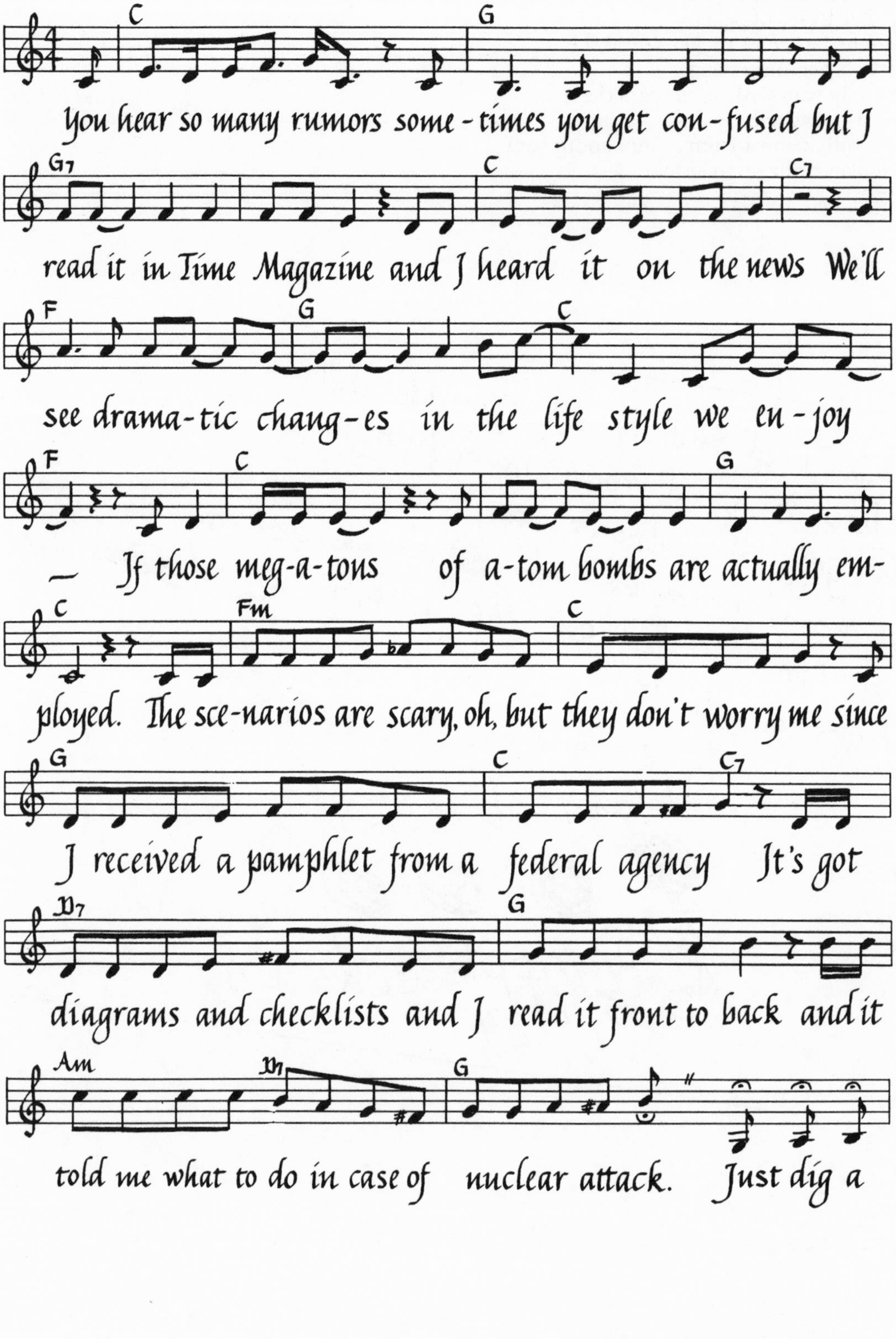

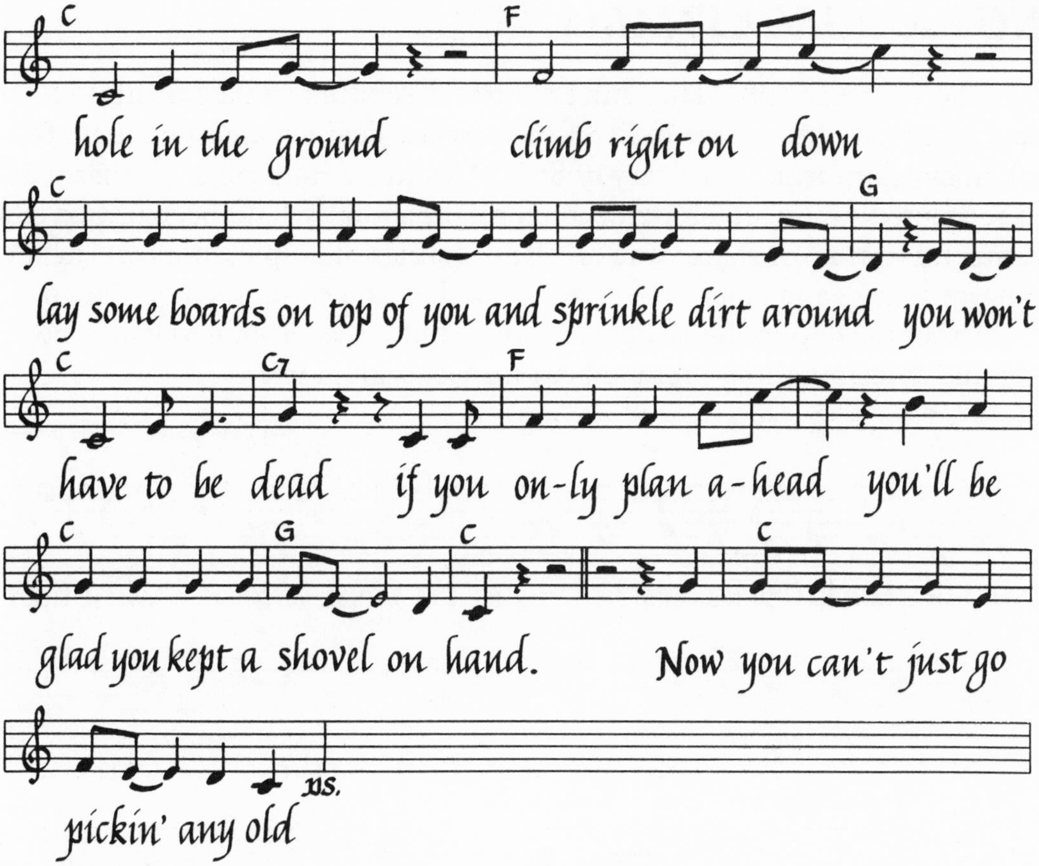

You hear so many rumors, sometimes you get confused
But I read it in Time Magazine and I saw it on the news
We'll see dramatic changes in the lifestyle we enjoy
If those megatons of atom bombs are actually employed

The scenarios are scary, oh, but they don't worry me
Since I received a pamphlet from a federal agency
It's got diagrams and checklists and I read it front to back
And it told me what to do in case of nuclear attack: Just

CHORUS:
Dig a hole in the ground, climb right on down
Lay some boards on top of you and sprinkle dirt around
You won't have to be dead if you only plan ahead
You'll be glad you kept a shovel on hand!

Now you can't just go picking any old place to dig your hole
Got to take a ride to the countryside to the town where you are told
If your plates are odd-numbered please don't panic, you'll be fine
Just politely let those even-numbered cars go first in line

If you don't have a car, just hail a cab or ride your bike
You can climb aboard the Amtrak train, sit back, and enjoy the sights
You and thousands of your city friends will be welcomed cordially
By townfolk who will show you country hospitality—then

CHORUS

We're sure to give you notice up to seven days before
But it's wise to recognize the warning signs of nuclear war
If the temperature is rising in a flash of blinding light
Grab your toothbrush and a flashlight and shut the windows tight

If the wind is blowing wicked and there's buildings in the air
Blisters on your body, fire in your hair
If the tupperware is melting and your dinner plans are wrecked
Stay calm, it's time to put this foolproof plan into effect: Just

CHORUS

NO MORE VIETNAMS

It is the winter of 1981. The United States is sending its best military technology to a minority regime in El Salvador while death squads decimate the civilian opposition and Secretary of State Alexander Haig suggests that the four murdered American churchwomen might actually have been armed combatants. It is a time of shame and rage and feelings of helplessness and deja vu. But peace groups and labor unions and churches and students mobilize to prevent further escalation. I sing at their rallies but I need a song to voice their anger and determination. I remember Phil Ochs, and I write.

© 1981 Pine Barrens Music (BMI)

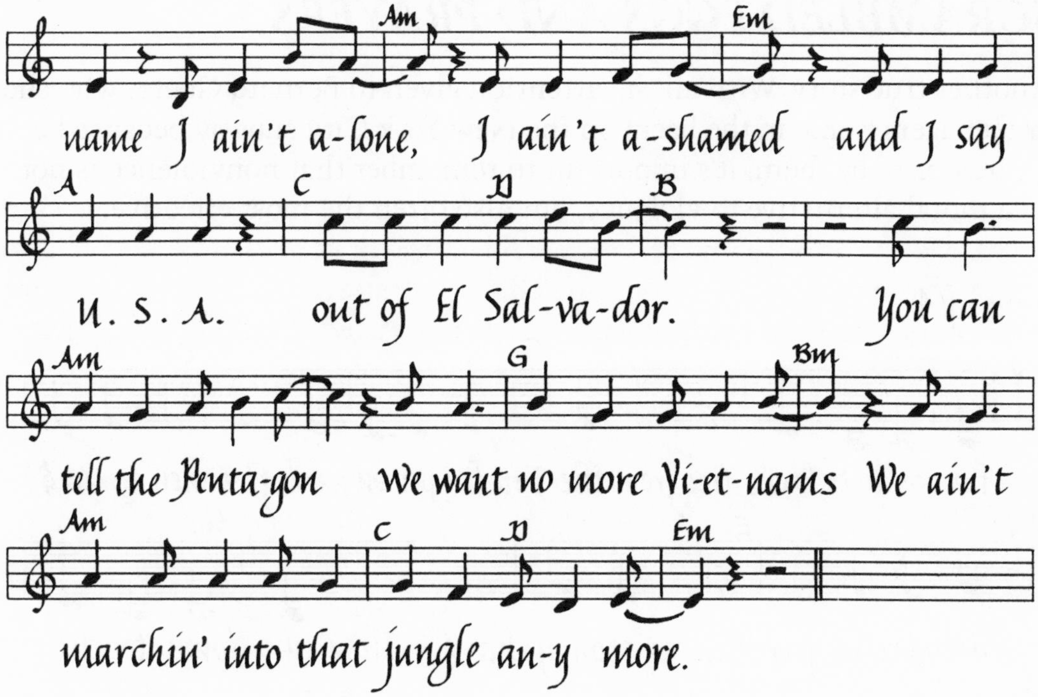

The marketplace was bustling in the morning
When the army and the ORDEN made their strike
Like a farmer killing chickens for the market
They cut down every living thing in sight
They tore into the wombs of the women
The sunlight gleaming on their bayonets
And the fishermen downstream though they never heard the screams
Hauled in a harvest of human carnage in their nets.

CHORUS:
Take down my name
I ain't alone, I ain't ashamed
And I say U.S.A. out of El Salvador!
You can tell the Pentagon we want no more Vietnams
We ain't marching into that jungle anymore.

She left her home in Ohio far behind her
She swore a sacred vow to help the poor
With three sisters she was raped and slowly tortured
Left in a shallow grave in El Salvador.
A doctor, he would grieve at all the suffering
He never asked his patient's party line
But he saved a rebel's life—the death squad came at night
Healing the sick his only crime.

CHORUS
Our taxes buy the bullets of the killers
Our helicopters darken southern skies
Our business wants new markets and cheap labor
Our papers rush to print C.I.A. lies
But take a message to the smiling politicians
Who like to talk so tough and act so brave
The rattling words of war, we've heard them all before
And we will answer them with peace and joy and rage.

CHORUS

SCRAMBLED EGGS AND PRAYERS

Another true story. With all the attention given to Bernard Goetz, who shot four teenagers (some in the back) on the New York City subway because he felt threatened by them, it's important to remember that nonviolence is not only a moral alternative to violence, but also often the most effective.

Capo up 4

© 1985 Pine Barrens Music (BMI)

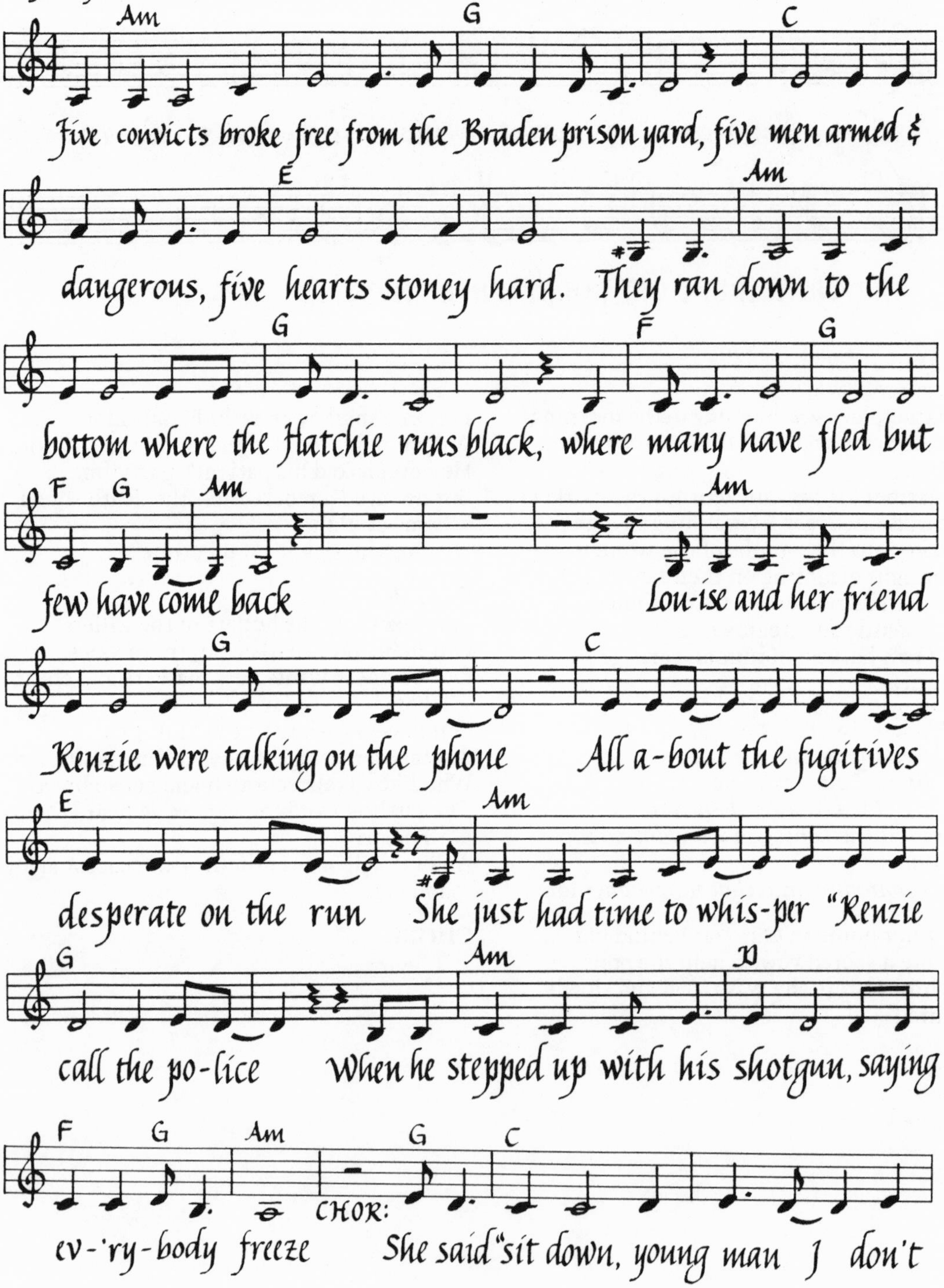

Five convicts broke free from the Braden prison yard
Five men armed and dangerous, five hearts stony hard
They ran down to the bottom where the Hatchie runs black
Where many have fled but few have come back
Louise and her friend Renzie were talking on the phone
All about the fugitives desperate on the run
She just had time to whisper, "Renzie, call the police"
When he stepped up with his shotgun, saying, "Everybody freeze."

CHORUS:
She said, "Sit down, young man, I don't want no violence here
I can see your body's weary and your soul laden with care
I'll cook you up some breakfast, you put that gun away.
Now sit down, young man, and pray."

He said, "Lady, I'm so hungry, I ain't eaten for three days"
She took out her skillet, fixed him bacon, bread, and eggs.
She talked about the bible, eyes crinkled when she smiled
He set down that shotgun and obeyed her like a child
She said, "Where is your mother?" He said, "I wish I knew."
She said, "I know your mother is praying for you.
I'm seventy-three years old, raised two boys of my own
And I know we must face judgment when we have done wrong."

CHORUS

He heard the cruiser coming, the cops were at the door
He looked out the window, said, "They'll kill me now for sure."
She said, "Finish up your breakfast, I'll let them do no harm."
He left the shotgun on the sofa and surrendered unarmed.
Now some folks might have meekly done whatever he had said
And some folks might have jumped him and probably turned up dead
You can tell it to your daughters and teach it to your sons
That scrambled eggs and prayers are stronger than guns.

CHORUS

SONGS OF LOVE & FRIENDSHIP

WILLIE'S SONG

I met Willie Sordill in 1974 when I was a first year law student in Ann Arbor, Michigan, and he was teaching at an alternative elementary school in Fort Wayne, Indiana, called The Learning Center. My boyhood friend, Sox Sperry, was also teaching there, and since he was the only other soul I then knew in the Midwest, naturally I visited him soon after I arrived. Willie and I hit it off and performed together at a tiny coffeehouse in Fort Wayne called The Lyre—Willie's first public performance as a guitarist and singer. We jammed on old favorites like "Don't Think Twice," "The Last Thing on My Mind," and "All Along the Watchtower." Over the years we became good friends.

Willie quit his teaching job, moved east to Cambridge, and soon organized the historic album of men's music, *Walls to Roses*. I moved to Cambridge soon afterward. In 1982 Willie's performing career took him on a national tour of nearly four months. His friends at home missed him, and while he was gone I wrote this song.

© 1983 Pine Barrens Music (BMI)

Lately you been traveling more than you are here
As your dreams describe a circle growing year by year
The postcard you send from Vancouver or South Bend
Recalls the friend too long away.

CHORUS:
May the rain run off your shoulder when you're caught in a storm
When the frost comes a-calling may it find you safe and warm
May your place be set, may your promises be kept,
May you never forget you are loved.

It was storming in Seattle when your car wouldn't start
Sunny in Salinas, where you nearly broke your heart
It was snowing in St. Paul but the people filled the hall
And you sent them all home singing through the cold.

CHORUS

Night falls hard in a faraway place
When you never knew the name and you can't recall the face
Your timing's off, you're tired, you can't imagine why they hired you
We are there in the silence by your side.

CHORUS

Fred and his Grandfather, 1956.

LIFEBOAT

There is something about the timeless power of the sea that touches our deepest feelings. I wrote this love song shortly after a volunteer stint on the Hudson River sloop *Clearwater,* when a sturdy ship meant comfort and safety.

Capo up 2

© 1981 Pine Barrens Music (BMI)

The times were lean, your eyes were bold
And we fell right in together like beggars on the road
And as the months turn into years with the passing of each day
It gets harder all the time to find a reason not to stay.

CHORUS

And when I need a lifeboat to keep out the sea
You are canvas and oak and you cradle me
And when I need a lifeboat and it looks like a storm
You are rudder and sail and you take me home.

Didn't need always to be strong
And when fear boiled up in anger, it never lasted long
It's a proud and reckless sailor who steers into the squall
But it's your arms that close around me as the rain begins to fall.

CHORUS

Knowing you, knowing me
Seems like we can be together, and we can still be free
And with every changing season I see deeper in your heart
And the memory stays with me when it's time to be apart.

LAST CHORUS

And when you need a lifeboat to keep out the sea
I am canvas and oak and you lean on me
And when you need a lifeboat and it looks like a storm
I am rudder and sail and I'll take you home.

Tuning up for a Clearwater sloop concert on the Westport, CT waterfront, 1975.

GONNA GET A GRANT

The public-interest version of the Beach Boys' "Wouldn't It Be Nice?"

Capo up 2

© 1981 Pine Barrens Music (BMI)

Ooh I can't get out of bed
Let's stay at home instead
I just want to play with you all day
Good loving gives me a thrill
But it don't pay the bills
Somehow true love will find a way.

CHORUS:
Gonna get a grant! Gonna get a grant!
Gonna get a grant to be in love
We'll philander for philanthropy
Doing what comes naturally
Let's get a grant for love!

Yum yum, we sure can cook
It's time we wrote the book
The whole world needs our recipe
We'll cuddle without a care
In our own endowed chair
In applied anthropology.

BRIDGE

Won't need no advanced degrees
We'll show 'em how we hug and squeeze
Kisses so delectable
They've got to be tax-deductible.

CHORUS

From Berkeley to M.I.T.
We'll be our favorite charity
Donating our bodies to research
We'll hit the best resorts
Sending quarterly reports
Graphing every lesson we have learned.

BRIDGE

Your methods drive me mad
I want to fund you so bad
And when our passion's sated
We can be evaluated!

CHORUS

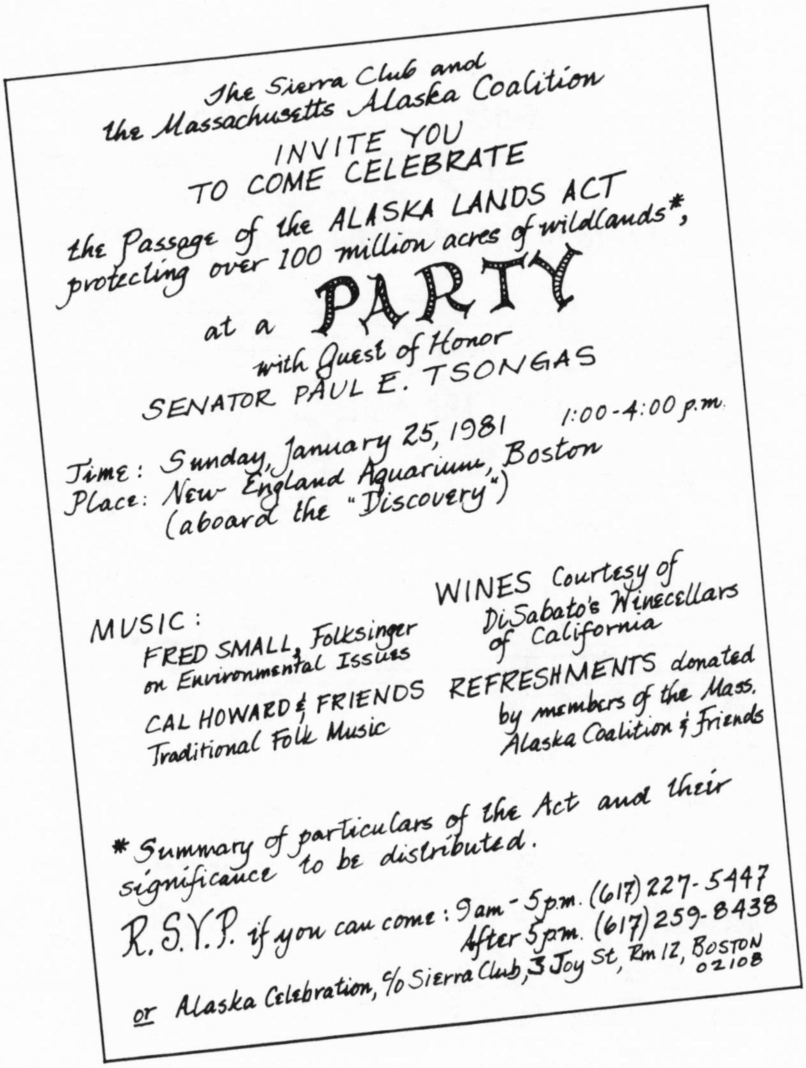
The Sierra Club and
the Massachusetts Alaska Coalition
INVITE YOU
TO COME CELEBRATE
the Passage of the ALASKA LANDS ACT
protecting over 100 million acres of wildlands*,
at a PARTY
with Guest of Honor
SENATOR PAUL E. TSONGAS

Time: Sunday, January 25, 1981 1:00-4:00 p.m.
Place: New England Aquarium, Boston
(aboard the "Discovery")

MUSIC:
FRED SMALL, Folksinger on Environmental Issues
CAL HOWARD & FRIENDS Traditional Folk Music

WINES Courtesy of DiSabato's Winecellars of California

REFRESHMENTS donated by members of the Mass. Alaska Coalition & Friends

* Summary of particulars of the Act and their significance to be distributed.

R.S.V.P. if you can come: 9am - 5pm. (617) 227-5447
After 5pm. (617) 259-8438
or Alaska Celebration, c/o Sierra Club, 3 Joy St, Rm 12, Boston 02108

CROSSING THE CHARLES

The view from the Longfellow Bridge between Cambridge and Boston is breathtakingly beautiful. Even at a sad time. Especially at a sad time.

Capo up 2

© 1981 Pine Barrens Music (BMI)

I guess it must say something
That I was the last to know
I never saw the signals flashing danger
Falling out of love with me
Was hard on you I know
To wake up in the morning to a stranger.

CHORUS:
Crossing the Charles the water's shining
And the sailboats running free
On this dirty old river
Winding down to the sea
Hello to the rumbling city
Goodbye to the windy sky
Wonder when I'm gonna get over
your leaving.

Less than lovers, not quite friends
Waiting for the wound to mend
You still work your magic without trying
Funny how many memories
The shortest love can hold
A sight, a sound, a word can leave
me crying.

CHORUS

I've thought it over and over again
Looking for the one to blame
Down a darkened street leading nowhere
I've left behind the anger now
I'm riding out the pain
Still reaching out and wishing you would
be there.

CHORUS

1964

HOUSEWARMING

Equal time for long-term relationships. *Cf.* "The Dancing Light."

Capo up 3

© 1981 Pine Barrens Music (BMI)

Brick and wood, mortar and plane
Labor's love, a little faith
You can see the structure taking form.
Ancient tools, a new design
Taking care, taking time
We've seen so many houses fall before.

CHORUS:
We are building a house growing tall before our eyes
Stone on stone, watch it rise
We are building a house with our hands, with our songs
May it stand as long as our lives.

As we tinker with the plans
Gentle friends lend their hands
Laying down a sturdy hardwood floor
For the future, from the past
Room to change, built to last
Come the snows of winter we'll be warm.

CHORUS

BRIDGE

And sometimes you'll need a vacation (I'll need one too)
Sunning on the sand, running in a blinding rain.
After the recreation
We can sleep in our own bed once again.

That easy chair you've always known
Photographs from long ago
Thanksgiving Day parade moving in
So many books upon the shelves
So much more to teach ourselves
Under this roof we shall begin.

CHORUS

SONGS OF STRUGGLE & CELEBRATION

LOVE'S GONNA CARRY US

And it does, over and over.

Open G tuning

© 1981 Pine Barrens Music (BMI)

CHORUS
It's been a long hard time
It's gonna be a long steep climb
But no one's gonna change our minds
'Bout what we gotta do
And when the road gets rough
Everybody's saying,"Just give it up"
All of our friends' sweet love
Gonna carry us through

We don't have the money
But we got the will
We got voices talking the truth
That can never be stilled
But they're gonna threaten
You know they have killed to get their way
But this movement we are building
Will not go away.

CHORUS

Beware of the heroes
Beware of the stars
'Cause a victory is hollow
If it ain't really ours
We're talking 'bout changes
Not just changing the faces at the top
They say that freedom is a constant struggle
And you can't ever stop.

CHORUS

Now we're gonna argue
We won't always agree
But we can't let anger blind us
To all we can be
Cause we need the laughter
And we need the tears to wash us clean
We need sisters and brothers beside us
To follow the dream

CHORUS

Photo: Todd Gipstein

Captain of the Taft School varsity football team, after a defeat, 1969.

STAND UP

A rally song, simple and singable. Of course, you don't have to physically "stand up" to take a stand. Just ask Rosa Parks.

© 1981 Pine Barrens Music (BMI)

The world has gone crazy, the country's a mess
You open your eyes and you just get depressed
If you take what they give you, they'll keep all the rest
Stand up and tell 'em you're here!

CHORUS:
Stand up, stand up and tell 'em you're here
Shout it out loud for the whole world to hear
They're long overdue for a kick in the rear
Stand up and tell 'em you're here!

Oh, the problems are so hard and talk is
so cheap
Counting the crises is like counting sheep
You can count on the experts and go back to
sleep
Or stand up and tell 'em you're here!

CHORUS

When you're fed up with being ignored and
abused
You're a mighty big bomb with a mighty
short fuse
Yes, we'll make 'em an offer they cannot
refuse
When we stand up and tell 'em we're here.

CHORUS*(. . . tell 'em we're here . . .)*

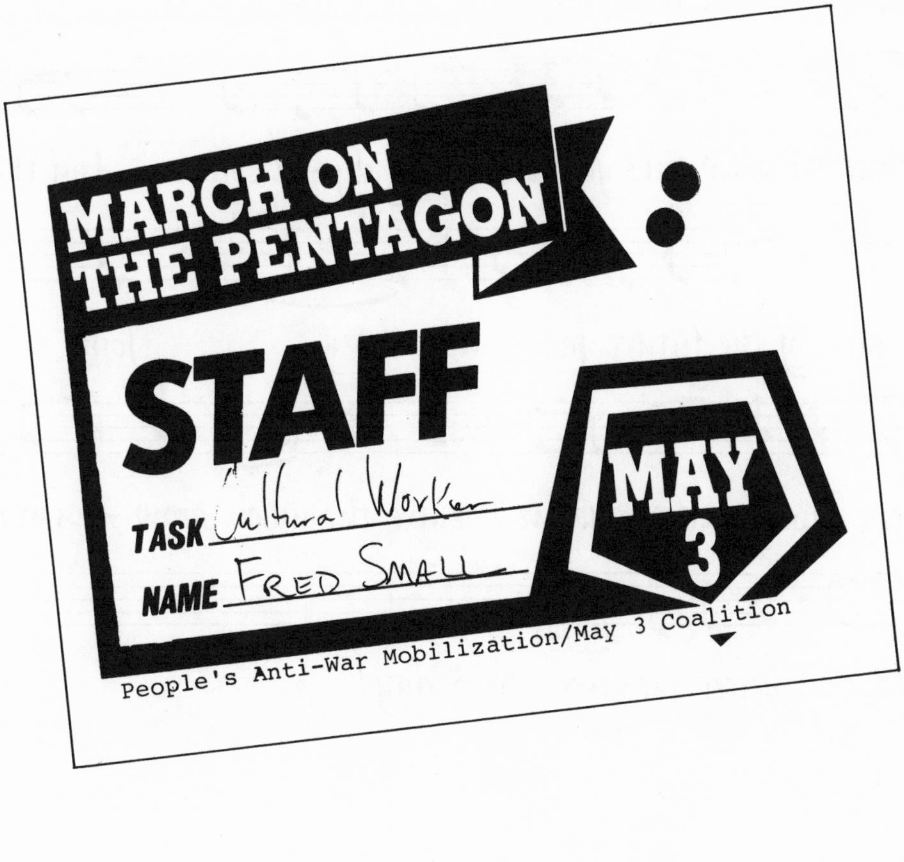

JOIN EVERY HAND (OCAW ORGANIZING SONG)

After hearing my song, "Death in Disguise" on WBAI in New York City, Shoptalk Productions asked me to write a song for the Oil, Chemical & Atomic Workers organizing slide show then in production. I wrote the song from tape-recorded interviews with OCAW field organizers describing their challenges and victories fighting for the right to a safe and healthy workplace and a decent wage.

© 1978 Fred Small

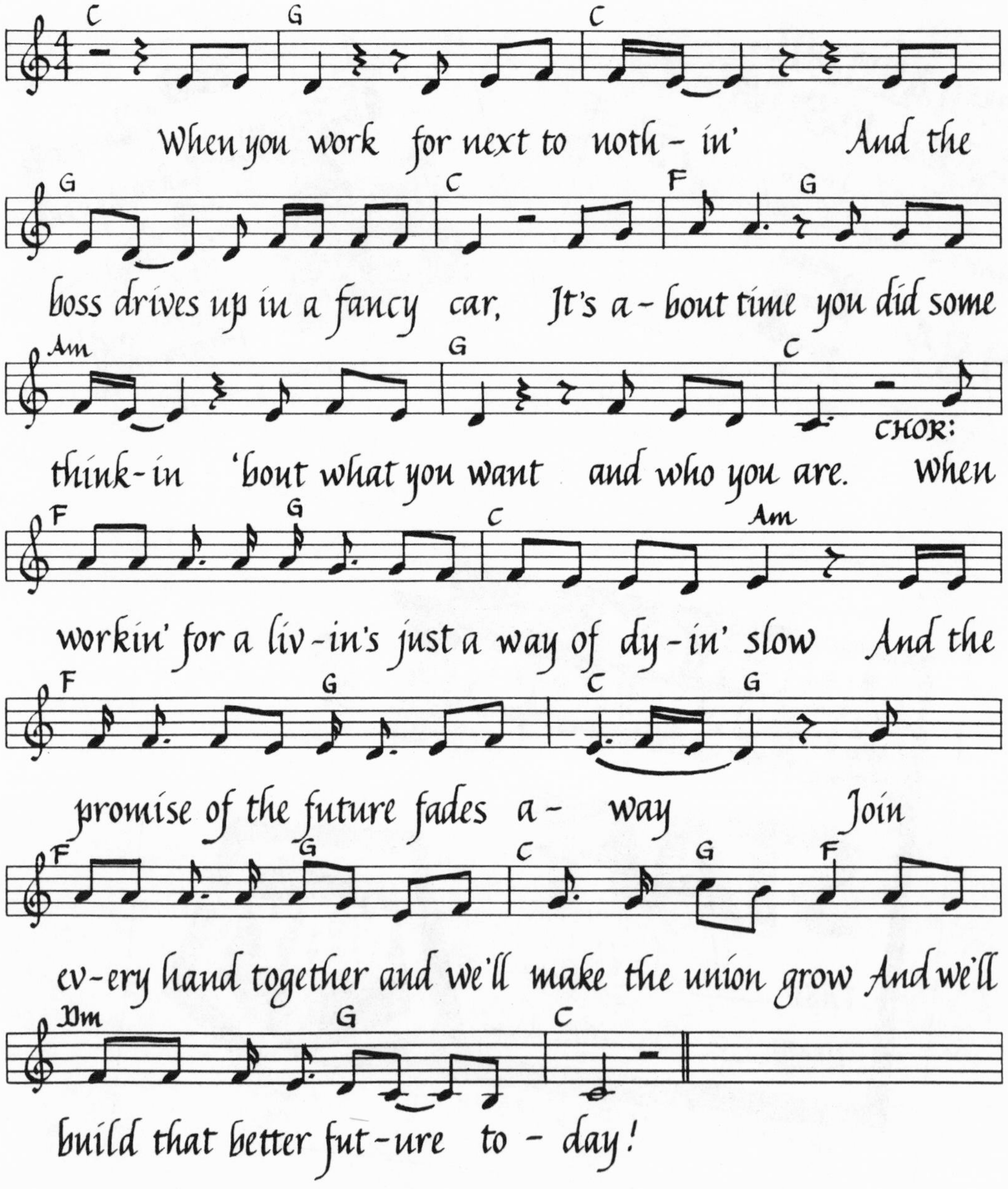

When you work for next to nothing
And the boss drives up in a fancy car,
It's about time you did some thinking
'Bout what you want and who you are.

You can ask and get no answer,
You can beg and they'll throw you a bone,
But if you want respect, if you want power,
You can't do it, you can't do it on your own.

CHORUS:
When working for a living's just a way of dying slow,
And the promise of the future fades away—
Join every hand together and we'll make the union grow
And we'll build that better future today!

America can't do without chemicals,
And it needs energy to make things go.
But when our work is so damn vital,
Why are our wages so damn low?

Unsafe conditions, equipment shoddy,
Dust and smoke burning your eyes—
You can give the boss your soul and body
And the boss'll give you the same old lies.

CHORUS

The boss'll sing and dance and he'll jump and holler,
Smile so sweetly and pitifully plead—
Oh, he'll say anything for his almighty dollar,
To keep the power from you and me.

And he will try to keep us divided,
Men from women, black from white.
Well, it's no wonder the boss gets all excited—
He knows how strong we will be when we unite.

CHORUS

Course, there ain't never been no shortcuts to freedom.
The struggle's hard—you know it's up to you.
But you'll be making your own decisions
Backed by the muscle of the OCAW.

So talk to your friends, talk to your neighbor—
Share your stories, share your gripes.
Share your courage, and do yourself a favor—
Don't wait no longer, the time is right!

CHORUS

"Some songs mainly help people forget their troubles. Others help people understand their troubles. Some few songs inspire people to do something about their troubles."

—Pete Seeger, *The Incompleat Folksinger*

FACE AT THE WINDOW

Government intrusion or social coercion of people's reproductive choices, sex lives, or private fantasies is neither conservatism nor radicalism, but fascism. I wrote this song in anticipation of the National Abortion Rights Action League's rally in Cherry Hill, New Jersey, in July 1982, but my thoughts and fears radiated far beyond that important issue.

© 1983 Pine Barrens Music (BMI)

In the stillness of the alley waits a man
with an open blade
And he hurts the woman badly and within
her plants his seed
She can't shake the dirt and horror as the
seed takes root and grows
But the law now claims her body, the
doctor's door is closed
She goes back to another alley to a leering
butcher's blade
And the deal is dark and bloody in the crime
the law has made.

CHORUS:

*And the face at the window never blinks
never looks away
When you wake in the night to a flashing
light
When you burn on judgment day
They have spoke aloud your daydreams
they have listened to your plans
They have watched you dance in the
rainstorm
They have seen you ride the wind.*

Walking slowly home at night a man
touching a man
And the car looks kind of familiar and it's
coming round again
You got no chance in that deadly dance
when they cut you to the bone
There's a bleeding gash from the broken
glass and you hear somebody moan
And maybe somebody calls the cops and
they take their own sweet time
And they say it's just a couple of fags again
and maybe your friend is dying.

CHORUS

And your lover comes to you softly and you
touch and you feel no shame
And you steal away from the city and
lightning fills your veins
In an air-conditioned office the committee
discusses your case
They know the words you whispered they
felt the flush upon your face

They have files on every fantasy, who's on
top and who's below
You have crossed into the shadow place
where outlaws freely roam.

CHORUS

You can drink the lies of paradise while the
books on the shelves disappear
You can make a comfortable living, you can
swear it can't happen here
And maybe they'll come for the unionists
and maybe they'll come for the Jews
And maybe they'll come for the heretics but
they'll never come for you
When you hear the step in the hallway,
when you taste the iron fear
Don't you go shouting out for justice 'cause
there's no one left to hear.

CHORUS

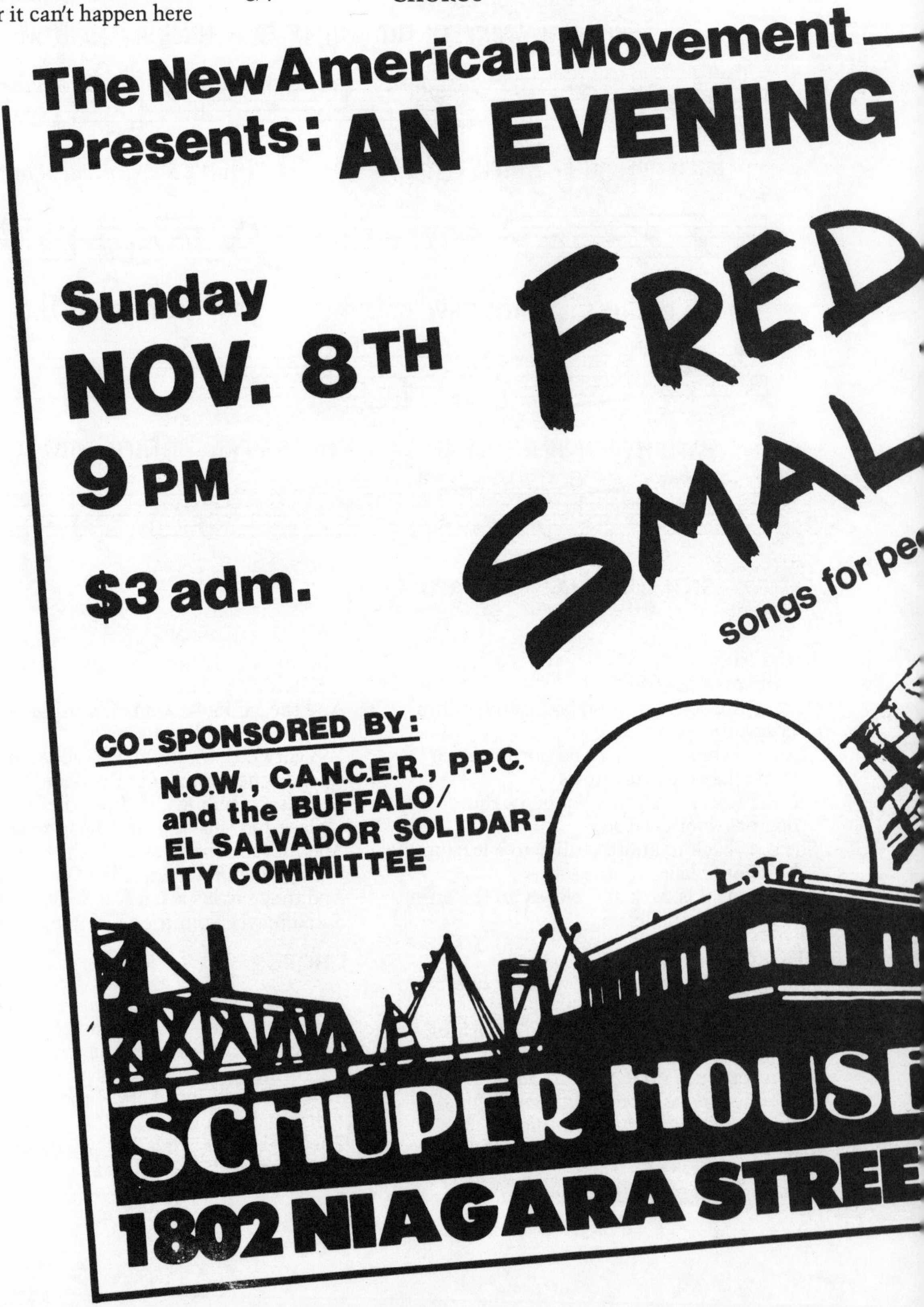

TH
GREAT
ARROW
GRAPHICS

NO LIMIT

A song of joy and possibility.

© 1985 Pine Barrens Music (BMI)

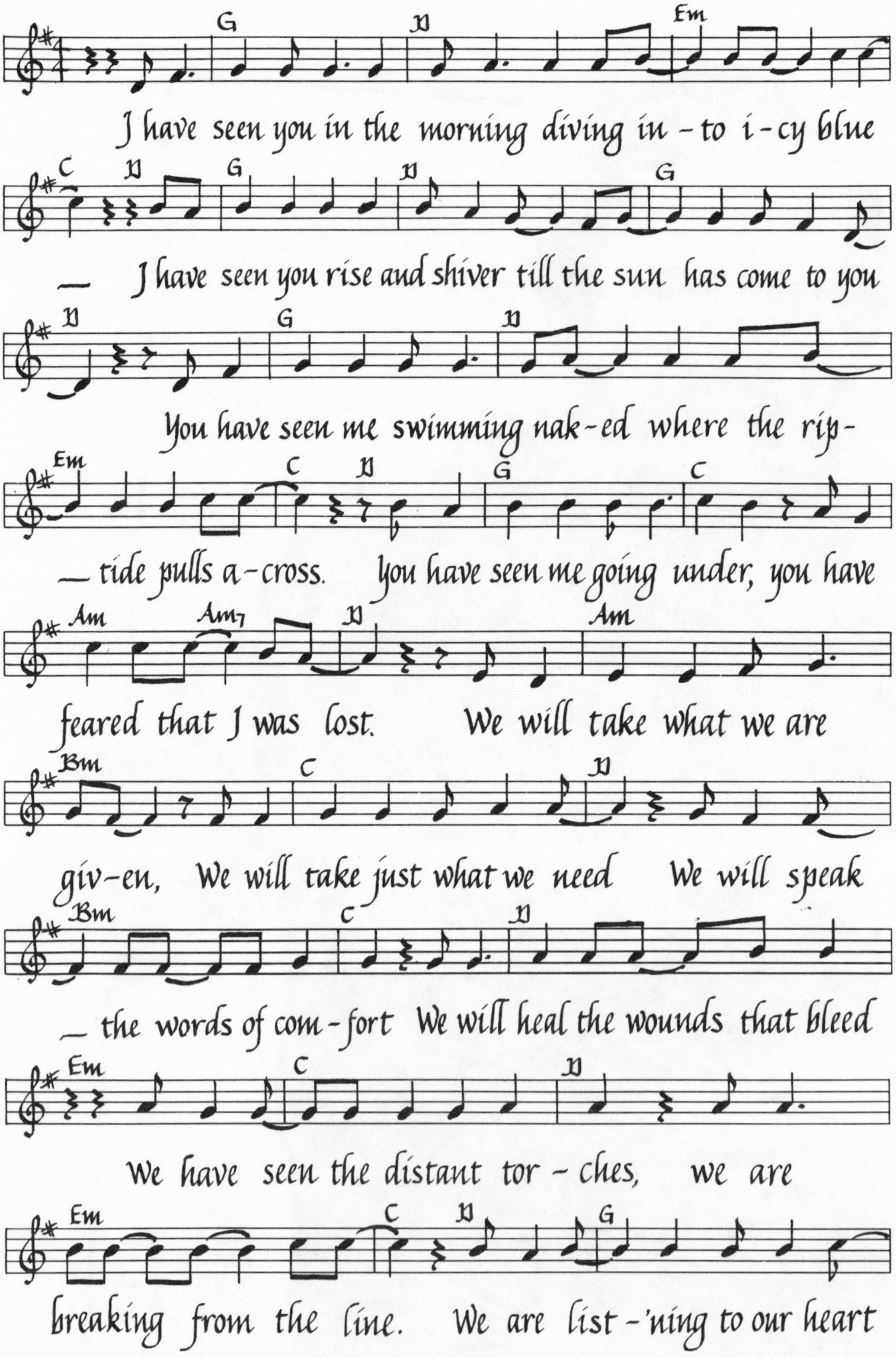

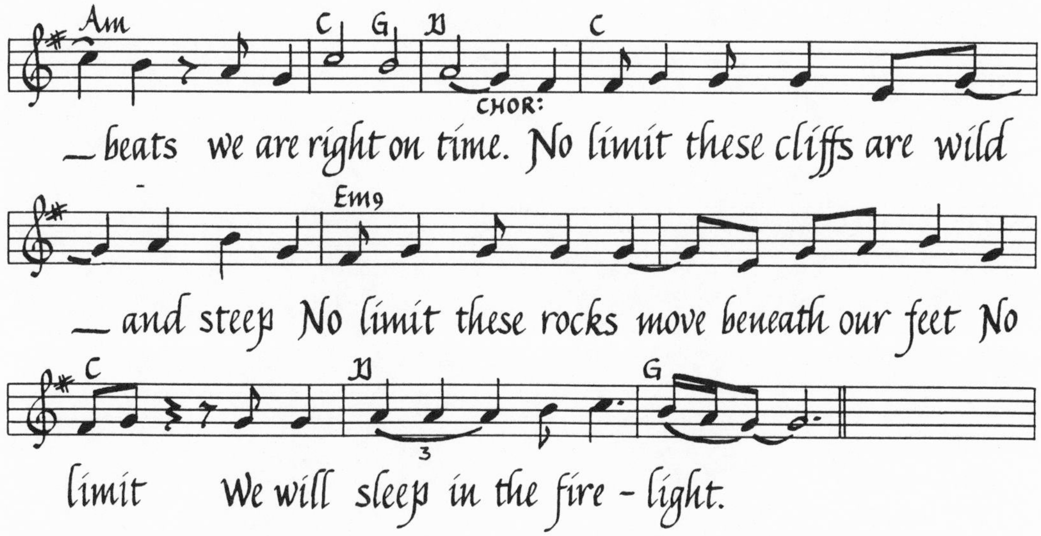

I have seen you in the morning diving into icy blue
I have seen you rise and shiver till the sun has come to you
You have seen me swimming naked where the riptide pulls across
You have seen me going under you have feared that I was lost
We will take what we are given we will take just what we need
We will speak the words of comfort we will heal the wounds that bleed
We have seen the distant torches we are breaking from the line
We are listening to our heartbeats we are right on time

No limit these cliffs are wild and steep
No limit these rocks move beneath our feet
No limit we will sleep in the firelight

I asked my sisters they said we are shining we are strong
Neither you nor we can navigate this wilderness alone
We are surrounded by the souls of those we love
We are unbounded we are here we are enough
I asked my brothers they said we have wanted your embrace
Your heart has been a fortress your words a state of seige
We will gather in the harvest with the strength of honest men
We will speak in awkward wonder we will weep we will begin

No limit no monkey on my back
No limit no slipping through the cracks
No limit no turning back no turning back

Those who chafe under their bondage know these chains have many links
Death is slender as a needle it is cool as just one drink
It is feeding on the silence it is strong with hateful words
It is massing on the border it is a sudden flight of birds
We will sing the songs of childhood we will dance the steps unknown
We will weave in blazing colors, we will let our terror show
We will call out to each other at the hour of attack
We are safe within our magic we will turn the demon back

No limit we are not what we seem
No limit we fly in our dreams
No limit we are brave and bright
No limit we are sound and light
No limit we are taking flight tonight

RESOURCE DIRECTORY

The people and publications listed here have been very helpful to me, and I find I am often hunting for their addresses to share with others. So for your convenience (and mine), here they are in one place.—Fred

Organizations

Building Bridges
P.O. Box 461
Cambridge, MA 02140

An organization that offers concerts and workshops on building personal relationships and political alliances between women and men and people of color and whites.

Hey Rube!
P.O. Box 9693
Minneapolis, MN 55440
(612) 333-2004

An association of performing artists in the folk tradition. A national gig list and health insurance are available.

National Organization for Changing Men
Box 93
Charleston, IL 61920

An organization of men challenging sexism, homophobia, and the ways in which men and women are denied our complete humanity.

People's Music Network
158 Cliff Street
Norwich, CT 06360

A network of people who make or support music that nourishes and informs movements for peace and justice. Conferences twice a year with workshops and songswaps.

Songs for a Changing World
P.O. Box 637
Cambridge, MA 02139

A national community of support for the music of Fred Small.

Magazines

The Black Sheep Review
One Camp Street
Cambridge, MA 02140
(617) 491-4435

Articles, reviews, songs, gossip, and even recipes of the folk music community of New England, the northeastern states, and beyond.

Broadside
P.O. Box 1464
New York, NY 10023

"The National Topical Song Magazine" that published Dylan's, Ochs's, and Paxton's first efforts is still going strong.

Changing Men
306 N. Brooks
Madison, WI 53715

Formerly "M." magazine, this journal publishes articles of interest to the profeminist men's movement.

Fast Folk Musical Magazine
178 W. Houston St. #9
New York, NY 10014

This magazine is actually a twelve-inch LP with the latest offerings from the New York folk crowd and others. Published kind of monthly.

Sing Out!
106 N. 4th Street
Box 1071
Easton, PA 18044
(215) 253-8105

Mainstay of the sixties folk revival, it's refortified and still offering lots of songs and information about the national folk music scene.

Books

Getting Organized
by Stephanie Winston
Warner Books, 1981

Time and space management for all of us too busy to do anything about it.

How to Make and Sell Your Own Record
by Diane Sward Rapaport
The Headlands Press, 1979

An indispensable how-to guide to putting out a record without a record company contract. Everything from soup to nuts.

Grass Roots International Folk Resource Directory
Edited by Leslie Berman and Heather Wood
Grass Roots Productions, 1985

An extensive listing of folk clubs, festivals, publications, radio stations, record companies and numerous other resources in the U.S. and abroad.

Making a Show of It
by Ginny Berson
Redwood Records, 1980

A handy and practical guide to concert production.

Record Distributors

All the distributors listed here carry my albums. Most sell both to retail stores and directly to consumers by mail. Roundup is mail order only; Rounder distributes only to stores.

Horizon, Inc.
33 Richdale Ave., #211
Cambridge, MA 02140

Ladyslipper
602 W. Chapel Hill St.
Durham, NC 27701

Midwest Music, Inc.
207 East Buffalo St.
Suite 545
Milwaukee, WI 53202

Rounder Distribution
One Camp Street
Cambridge, MA 02140

Roundup Records
P.O. Box 154
N. Cambridge, MA 02140

Silo/Alcazar
S. Main St.,
Box 429
Waterbury, VT 05676

Other Music Resources

Broadcast Music, Inc. (BMI)
320 W. 57th St.
New York, NY 10019
(212) 586-2000

BMI, like its competitor ASCAP, collects and distributes broadcast royalties. (They don't seem to listen to folk music much!)

Copyright Office
Library of Congress
Washington, DC 20559
(202) 287-8700 (information)
(202) 287-9100 (forms only)

I've got my quarrels with the government, but the Copyright Office has always been friendly and helpful. For song copyright, ask for Form PA.

New Song Library
P.O. Box 295
Northhampton, MA 01061

This is a marvelous clearinghouse and repository for topical songs. You need a song, they'll find it!

NOTES ON THE CHORDS

Since I consider myself more a songwriter than an instrumentalist, I've been surprised and tickled when people have expressed a keen interest in how I play particular songs on the guitar. Space limitations preclude a comprehensive guide here, but I thought it might be useful to provide some of the chord formations I use. (If you want more details, grab me after a concert and I'll be happy to show you.)

I play most of my songs in standard concert tuning: the strings are tuned (from sixth to first) E-A-D-G-B-E. I use conventional folk-style chords, favoring these patterns:

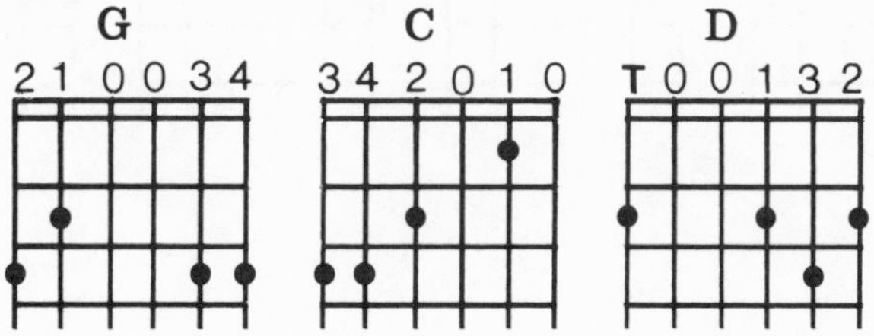

On "Cranes over Hiroshima," which I perform in the key of E, I usually choose these voicings for A and B (sounding all strings):

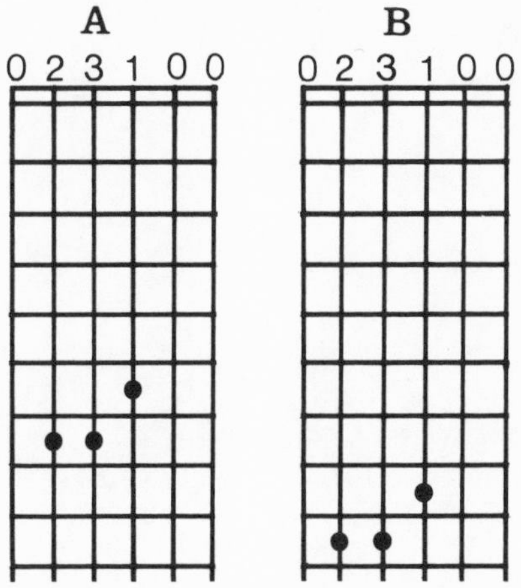

When I play in the key of D, I tune the sixth (bass) string down a whole step from E to D. This is called dropped-D tuning and gives a strong, rich sound. Here are some common chords in this tuning:

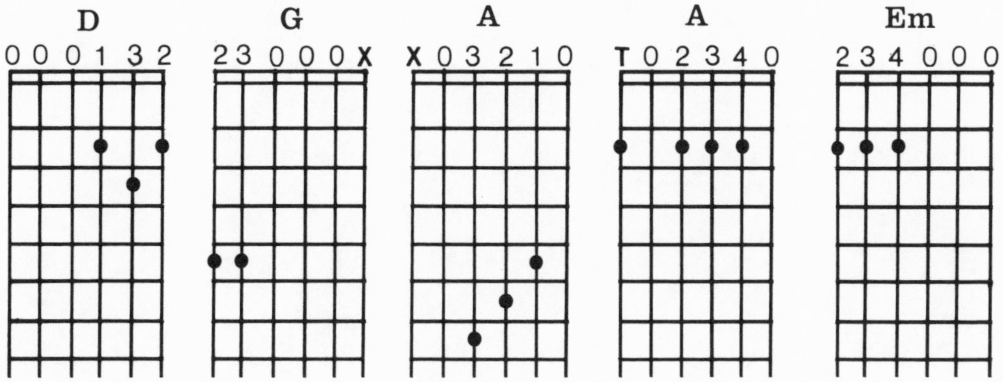

For "Love's Gonna Carry Us," I tune my guitar in open G: D-G-D-G-B-D. These basic chords are used in this tuning:

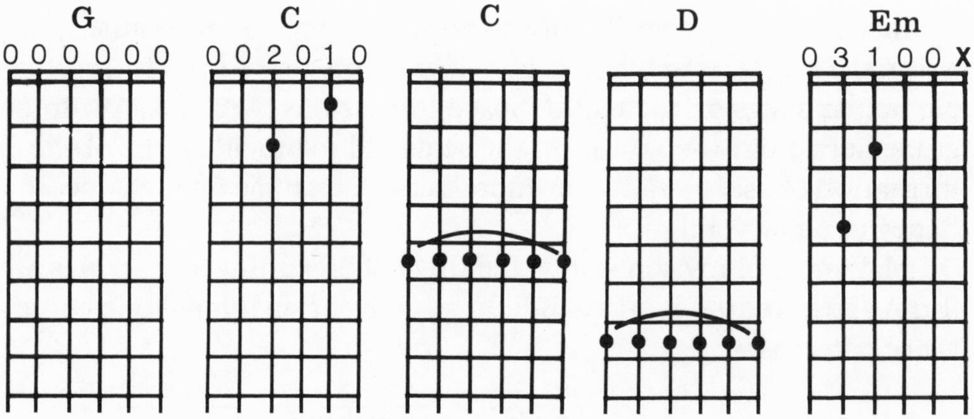

TITLE INDEX